Praise for *Prayer*

The church desperately needs to be called back to the place of truly seeking God's face and praying in God's kingdom. Few are more qualified to make that call than A.W. Tozer. And I know of no one more like Tozer and more able to communicate what Tozer would say today than Dr. Bill Seaver. I heartily recommend the thoughtful and prayerful reading of this book. As you do that, you will experience personal spiritual renewal along with a strong desire to see others receive the same.

GARY HUTCHISON
Senior Pastor, Grace Community Church
Arlington, Texas

It is a great delight and joy to commend this book on prayer. In this book of excerpts from A. W. Tozer's popular writings, Dr. Bill Seaver provides a great tool with clear directions for meditation and prayer. Few books are worth a second read, but this one goes on my shelf as one to get to know like a good friend.

GALE HARTLEY
Pastor, Bethany Baptist Church, Mountain City, Tennessee
Served in Eastern Europe with the International Mission Board of the Southern Baptist Convention

A. W. Tozer was a mighty man of prayer. Dr. Seaver leads us into a deep understanding of this revealing, convicting, and powerful life of dynamic prayer. This type of prayer weaves for us a seamless tapestry of sweet communion with our Father and sacrificial service to one another.

BRUCE ALLSOP, MD
Family Medicine, Trinity Counseling Center, Knoxville, Tennessee
Association of Certified Biblical Counseling

PRAYER

PRAYER

COMMUNING WITH GOD IN EVERYTHING—
COLLECTED INSIGHTS FROM

A. W. TOZER

COMPILED BY W. L. SEAVER

MOODY PUBLISHERS
CHICAGO

Edited by James Vincent
Interior and Cover design: Erik M. Peterson
Cover art by Unhidden Media, unhiddenmedia.com

Library of Congress Cataloging-in-Publication Data

Names: Tozer, A. W. (Aiden Wilson), 1897-1963. | Seaver, W. L., compiler.
Title: Prayer : communing with God in everything--collected insights from A.
   W. Tozer / compiled by W.L. Seaver.
Description: Chicago : Moody Publishers, 2016. | Includes bibliographical
   references.
Identifiers: LCCN 2015034041 | ISBN 9780802413819
Subjects: LCSH: Prayer--Christianity.
Classification: LCC BV210.3 .T69 2016 | DDC 248.3/2--dc23 LC record available at
http://lccn.loc.gov/2015034041

We hope you enjoy this book from Moody Publishers. Our goal is to provide high-quality, thought-provoking books and products that connect truth to your real needs and challenges. For more information on other books and products written and produced from a biblical perspective, go to www.moodypublishers.com or write to:

Moody Publishers
820 N. LaSalle Boulevard
Chicago, IL 60610

5 7 9 10 8 6 4

Printed in the United States of America

To my beautiful wife, Barbara,
and to my family and friends,
who were truly my prayer partners
from the inception to the completion of this work,
and to my God, who divinely enabled me to pen this work.

CONTENTS

TOZER SERMONS

Introduction

A JOURNEY AWAITS

With fear and trembling, I approached this task of compiling Tozer's words on prayer and praying. I tried to avoid it, but the Spirit kept drawing me back to the riches of the topic for myself and others. While I did complete one of the first courses on prayer taught at a seminary over thirty years ago, the biggest plus of that experience was the opportunity to read a lot of books on prayer by Andrew Murray, E. M. Bounds, Ole Hallesby, D. L. Moody, Watchman Nee, Leonard Ravenhill, and others. In the years to follow there were successes and failures in my prayer life, but I know that the priority of prayer and the Word of God (Acts 6:4) should still hold today for all saints.

When one peruses the writings of Tozer on prayer, one does not find how-to manuals on prayer or exposition of famous prayers of the saints in the Bible from Abraham to David to Daniel and to the minor prophets, nor from Stephen outside

Jerusalem to Paul in Rome. The reason for these omissions may be found in Tozer's words in his book, *The Counselor*:

> Do you recall that in the times of prayer recorded in the Gospels the only one who could stay awake was Jesus? Others tried to pray, but they came to Him and said, "Teach us to pray" (Luke 11:1).
>
> Some of the churches now advertise courses on how to pray. How ridiculous! That is like giving a course on how to fall in love. When the Holy Spirit comes He takes the things of God and translates them into language our hearts can understand. Even if we do not know the will of God, the Holy Spirit does know, and He prays "with groanings which cannot be uttered" (Rom. 8:26). These disciples were praying people—in the book of Acts you will find them in prayer meetings. But before that, they would fall asleep. The difference was by the Spirit—now they had great delight in prayer.[1]

With that being said, it is fairly evident that Tozer dealt with the believer's daily relationship with the Lord and how that produced effective prayer.

For instance, such thoughts about the Christian's daily walk with the Lord and effective prayer come from studying Abraham's prayer for Sodom and Gomorrah where Lot was living, as recorded in Genesis 18:22–33:

> Then the men turned away from there and went toward Sodom, while Abraham was still standing before the Lord.

Abraham came near and said, "Will You indeed sweep away the righteous with the wicked?" Suppose there are fifty righteous within the city; will You indeed sweep it away and not spare the place for the sake of the fifty righteous who are in it? Far be it from You to do such a thing, to slay the righteous with the wicked, so that the righteous and the wicked are treated alike. Far be it from You! Shall not the Judge of all the earth deal justly?" So the Lord said, "If I find in Sodom fifty righteous within the city, then I will spare the whole place on their account." And Abraham replied, "Now behold, I have ventured to speak to the Lord, although I am but dust and ashes. Suppose the fifty righteous are lacking five, will You destroy the whole city because of five?" And He said, "I will not destroy it if I find forty-five there." He spoke to Him yet again and said, "Suppose forty are found there?" And He said, "I will not do it on account of the forty." Then he said, "Oh may the Lord not be angry, and I shall speak; suppose thirty are found there?" And He said, "I will not do it if I find thirty there." And he said, "Now behold, I have ventured to speak to the Lord; suppose twenty are found there?" And He said, "I will not destroy it on account of the twenty." Then he said, "Oh may the Lord not be angry, and I shall speak only this once; suppose ten are found there?" And He said, "I will not destroy it on account of the ten." As soon as He had finished speaking to Abraham the Lord departed, and Abraham returned to his place. (NASB)

I have studied this passage numerous times, and it is rich in principles on prayer. Later Abraham will be called a friend of God because of these events in Genesis 18 (Isa. 41:8; James 2:23). True friends don't hide revelations or issues from each other. God didn't hide from Abraham what He was going to do with Sodom and Gomorrah (see Gen. 18:17). As a result of God not hiding the truth, Abraham lingered before the Lord and prayed with much boldness, perseverance, and humility, for he knew God to be merciful and just.

His first petition was for God to spare Sodom and Gomorrah if there were fifty righteous people within the city, and his last one (five petitions later) was for God to spare the city if there were ten righteous. What is extremely interesting, there was an 80 percent change in the original petition from fifty righteous men to ten. Or another way to look at it was that there was an average of a 25 percent change in each petition from the previous petition. This snapshot of Abraham's prayer life reveals the spiritual journey that awaits those who linger before the Lord God as Abraham did.

A spiritual journey awaits us as God reshapes our petitions, molds us more into the image of His Son, and brings closure to the matter prayed about in such a way that His holiness, His mercy, His love, and His glory are ever magnified. If our everyday lives are filled with the barrenness of busyness and no serious urgency to pray, then we miss the wonderful journey of being conformed to the image of Christ and knowing our God more intimately.

This is the journey that Tozer addresses in his works and that we have tried to capture. But that journey begins with the choices we make! I pray that you may be very teachable in this journey and that your understanding of who God is may be greatly expanded. Blessings to you as a fellow sojourner!

Finally, the first twenty-two chapters of this book focus on Tozer's writings from sixteen books that deal with some aspect of prayer. The next three chapters are snippets from some sermons that deal with prayer and related topics. The last three chapters are excerpts from two major sermons that Tozer gave on prayer. To help us reflect and respond, each chapter concludes with a response section, "To Reflect and Apply," which includes questions and action steps. In addition, chapters one through twenty-five have a transition section, "Exploring with Tozer," that amplifies on Tozer's thoughts on the specific prayer topic. We have omitted the "Exploring with Tozer" section in Tozer's lengthier final prayer sermons.

The book can be used by the individual for personal reflection, by a small group for discussion, or as a monthly devotional on prayer. If you are using this book for devotional time on prayer, the twenty-two writings, three snippets, and three excerpts from Tozer's Sunday sermons will take you through twenty-eight days. The author and compiler of this material encourages the reader to go back to two of the most convicting chapters to finish the month's readings. However, it is very possible that the reader will spend two days on a chapter because of the richness of applications in that chapter that are pertinent to his/her situation.

May God incline your heart to pray more effectively and more pointedly in the days to come!

W. L. Seaver

1

THE WHOLE
LIFE MUST PRAY

Prayer at its best is the expression of the total life.

Certainly there have been and will continue to be instances when an isolated prayer may be answered even when the one uttering it may not have been living an exemplary Christian life. But we assume that most of those who read this page are not satisfied to get a prayer through occasionally; they want to know a more satisfying prayer life, one that elevates and purifies every act of body and mind and integrates the entire personality into a single spiritual unit. Such prayer can only be the result of a life lived in the Spirit.

All things else being equal, our prayers are only as powerful as our lives. In the long pull we pray only as well as we live. Some prayers are like a fire escape, used only in times of critical emergency—never very enjoyable, but used as a way of terrified escape from disaster. They do not represent the regular life of the one who offers them; rather they are the unusual and uncommon acts of the spiritual amateur.

William Law somewhere pleads for Christians to live lives that accord with their prayers, and one of our well-known hymns asks that God help us "to live more nearly as we pray." Most of us in moments of stress have wished that we had lived so that prayer would not be so unnatural to us and have regretted that we had not cultivated prayer to the point where it would be as easy and as natural as breathing.

We do not want to leave the impression that prayer in times of sudden crisis is not a good and right thing. It most certainly is, and God is said to be a "very present help in trouble" (Ps. 46:1); but no instructed Christian wants to live his whole life on an emergency level. As we go on into God we shall see the excellency of the life of constant communion where all thoughts and acts are prayers, and the entire life becomes one holy sacrifice of praise and worship.

To pray effectively it is required of us that there be no unblessed areas in our lives, nor parts of the mind or soul that are not inhabited by the Spirit, no impure desires allowed to live within us, no disparity between our prayers and our conduct.

All this may appear to be placing the standard too high to be reached by men and women under the sun. But it is not so. If Christ is the kind of Savior He claims to be, He should be able to save His people from the bondage of sin. This is not to support the man-made doctrine of "sinless perfection"; it is rather to declare the God-inspired doctrine that it is possible to "walk in the Spirit" and so "not fulfill the lust of the flesh." It is to say that God has made provision in the cross of Christ for His children to be delivered from the galling yoke of sin: "Likewise reckon ye also yourselves to be dead indeed unto sin, but alive unto God through Jesus Christ our Lord" (Rom. 6:11).

Undoubtedly the redemption in Christ Jesus has sufficient moral power to enable us to live in a state of purity and love where our whole life will be a prayer. Individual acts of prayer that spring out of that kind of total living will have about them a wondrous power not known to the careless or the worldly Christian.

From *The Root of the Righteous*
(1955; repr., Chicago: Moody, 2015)

EXPLORING WITH TOZER

Tozer's opening comment that "prayer at its best is the expression of the total life" is both a simple and complex truth. It is simple to the believer who is in constant communion with the Father where all his thoughts and acts are prayers. His entire life is one holy sacrifice of praise and worship. This individual is not necessarily a prayer warrior as others would classify him; but a saint desirous of moment by moment fellowship with the Lord, of impacting his world for Christ not only by his righteous actions but also his prayers, and of leaving the fragrance of Christ among believers and nonbelievers. This believer understands that God "always leads us in triumph in Christ" (2 Cor. 2:14–15).

The truth that "prayer at its best is the total expression of the total life" is complex to the believer who is not in constant communion with the Father, who has conformed much to the world, and who sees prayer only as a fire escape in difficult times or in critical emergencies. This believer tends to call on God only when he cannot work out a solution to a difficult situation, that is, he has no other option. To this believer, prayer is a duty and burdensome. "For this is the love of God, that we keep His commandments; and His commandments are not burdensome" (1 John 5:3). When the whole life prays, there is no burden or legalistic bondage with prayer. The other issue that adds to the complexity of this truth on the total life is the inability of this believer to discern or connect the dots on unanswered prayer, sin, and their walk in Christ. Prayer seems to be a mystery to this believer, a random process that doesn't make sense. However, in actuality, God is trying to grasp the attention of this believer by unanswered prayers or few prayers being answered to make him realize that God desires his submission to Him in all things under the power of the Holy Spirit, his resistance to the devil, and his drawing near to God (and God will draw near to him) (James 4:7–8). If this believer responds to God's wooing, he will begin to realize that a holy life is the fertile soil for prayer that changes the world around them. To not respond to God's gentle and loving promptings forces God the Father to discipline us in many ways inclusive of our prayers that we might share His holiness (Heb. 12:10). Thus, the journey is more painful and complex!

REFLECT AND APPLY

1. "All things being equal, our prayers are only as powerful as our lives." How does one assess our life in Christ? Do we start with prayer? Put another way, are my prayers filled with emergency prayers or much prayer throughout my day? Do we examine our priorities of seeking first the kingdom of God? This honest assessment will take some time alone and may require some input from a spiritual mentor or two.

2. How does one cultivate a prayer life so that prayer becomes as natural as breathing? Should we read more books on prayer? Talk about prayer more? Pray more? Study James 4:7–8; 1 Peter 5:6–10; and 2 Kings 22:18–20.

3. What were the circumstances of your last emergency prayer? What was the answer? How was your prayer life affected after that—did it become a digression, a return to the status quo, or serve as a progression? Write down your impressions of the aftereffects from your last answered emergency prayer.

4. Was there a time in your life where you prayed more or saw more answered prayer? Reflect on what your walk in Christ was like at that time. On the other hand, can you identify some times in your life where your walk in Christ was more holy but answered prayer was less? What is the possible reason for this?

2

THE SACRAMENT OF LIVING: PART 1

One of the greatest hindrances to internal peace the Christian encounters is the common habit of dividing our lives into two areas—the sacred and the secular. As these areas are conceived to exist apart from each other and to be morally and spiritually incompatible, and as we are compelled by the necessities of living to be always crossing back and forth from the one to the other, our inner lives tend to break up so that we live a divided instead of a unified life.

Our trouble springs from the fact that we who follow Christ inhabit at once two worlds—the spiritual and the natural. As children of Adam we live our lives on earth subject to the limitations of the flesh and the weaknesses and ills to which human nature is heir. Merely to live among men requires of us years of hard toil and much care and attention to the things of this world. In sharp contrast to this is our life in the Spirit. There we enjoy another and a higher kind of life—we are children of God; we possess heavenly status and enjoy intimate fellowship with Christ.

This tends to divide our total life into two departments. We come unconsciously to recognize two sets of actions. The first are performed with a feeling of satisfaction and a firm assurance that [these actions] are pleasing to God. These are the sacred acts and they are usually thought to be prayer, Bible reading, hymn singing, church attendance, and such other acts as spring directly from faith. They may be known by the fact that they have no direct relation to this world, and would have no meaning whatever except as faith shows us another world, "an house not made with hands, eternal in the heavens" (2 Cor. 5:1).

Over against these sacred acts are the secular ones. They include all of the ordinary activities of life we share with the sons and daughters of Adam: eating, sleeping, working, looking after the needs of the body, and performing our dull and prosaic duties here on earth. These we often do reluctantly and with many misgivings, often apologizing to God for what we consider a waste of time and strength. The upshot of this is that we are uneasy most of the time. We go about our common tasks with a feeling of deep frustration, telling ourselves pensively that there's a better day coming when we shall slough off this earthly shell and be bothered no more with the affairs of this world.

This is the old sacred-secular antithesis. Most Christians are caught in its trap. They cannot get a satisfactory adjustment between the claims of the two worlds. They try to walk the tightrope between two kingdoms and they find no peace in either.

Their strength is reduced, their outlook confused and their joy taken from them.

I believe this state of affairs to be wholly unnecessary. We have gotten ourselves on the horns of a dilemma, true enough, but the dilemma is not real. It is a creature of misunderstanding. The sacred-secular antithesis has no foundation in the New Testament. Without doubt, a more perfect understanding of Christian truth will deliver us from it.

The Lord Jesus Christ Himself is our perfect example, and He knew no divided life. In the presence of His Father He lived on earth without strain from babyhood to His death on the cross. God accepted the offering of His total life, and made no distinction between act and act. "I do always those things that please him" was His brief summary of His own life as it related to the Father (John 8:29). As He moved among men He was poised and restful. What pressure and suffering He endured grew out of His position as the world's sin bearer; they were never the result of moral uncertainty or spiritual maladjustment.

The apostle Paul's exhortation to "do all to the glory of God" is more than pious idealism. It is an integral part of the sacred revelation and is to be accepted as the very Word of Truth. It opens before us the possibility of making every act of our lives contribute to the glory of God. Lest we should be too timid to include everything, Paul mentions specifically eating and drinking. This humble privilege we share with the beasts that perish. If these lowly animal acts can be so performed as to honor God, then it becomes difficult to conceive of one that cannot.

That monkish hatred of the body, which figures so prominently in the works of certain early devotional writers, is wholly without support in the Word of God. Common modesty is found in the sacred Scriptures, it is true, but never prudery or a false sense of shame. The New Testament accepts as a matter of course that in His incarnation our Lord took upon Him a real human body, and no effort is made to steer around the downright implications of such a fact. He lived in that body here among men and never once performed a non-sacred act. His presence in human flesh sweeps away forever the evil notion that there is about the human body something innately offensive to the Deity. God created our bodies, and we do not offend Him by placing the responsibility where it belongs. He is not ashamed of the work of His own hands.

Perversion, misuse, and abuse of our human powers should give us cause enough to be ashamed. Bodily acts done in sin and contrary to nature can never honor God. Wherever the human will introduces moral evil we have no longer our innocent and harmless powers as God made them; we have instead an abused and twisted thing which can never bring glory to its Creator.

Let us, however, assume that perversion and abuse are not present. Let us think of a Christian believer in whose life the twin wonders of repentance and the new birth have been wrought. He is now living according to the will of God as he understands it from the written Word. Of such a one it may be said that every act of his life is or can be as truly sacred as prayer or baptism or the Lord's Supper. To say this is not to bring all acts down to one dead level; it is rather to lift every act up into a living kingdom and turn the whole life into a sacrament.

If a sacrament is an external expression of an inward grace, then we need not hesitate to accept the above thesis. By one act of consecration of our total selves to God we can make every subsequent act express that consecration. We need no more be ashamed of our body—the fleshly servant that carries us through life—than Jesus was of the humble beast upon which He rode into Jerusalem. "The Lord hath need of [him]" (Matt. 21:3) may well apply to our mortal bodies. If Christ dwells in us, we may hear about the Lord of glory as the little beast did of old and give occasion to the multitudes to cry, "Hosanna in the highest."

That we *see* this truth is not enough. If we would escape from the toils of the sacred-secular dilemma, the truth must "run in our blood" and condition the complex of our thoughts. We must practice living to the glory of God, actually and determinedly. By meditation upon this truth, by talking it over with God often in our prayers, by recalling it to our minds frequently as we move about among men, a sense of its wondrous meaning will take hold of us. The old painful duality will go down before a restful unity of life. The knowledge that we are all God's, that He has received all and rejected nothing, will unify our inner lives and make everything sacred to us.

From *The Pursuit of God*
(1948; repr., Chicago: Moody, 2015)

EXPLORING WITH TOZER

This particular selection from Tozer's works might seem a bit strange to be chosen for a book on prayer, especially since references to prayer are slight. However, Tozer makes it clear from the outset, as do the Scriptures, that "the common habit of dividing our lives into two areas—the sacred and the secular" is one of the greatest hindrances to internal peace for the Christian, who inhabits two worlds, the spiritual and the natural. This compartmentalization of life leads a believer to identify sacred acts, such as prayer, Bible study, worship, and more, and then to categorize the secular acts of everyday life as mundane and non-spiritual. Tozer notes that most Christians today are caught in this trap between two worlds. As a result, "they try to walk the tightrope between two kingdoms and they find no peace in either. Their strength is reduced, their outlook confused, and their joy taken from them."

This tension, this conflict, this uneasiness, or this dilemma can lead to a Christian life filled with powerlessness and prayerlessness. Every act of our lives should contribute to the glory of God, and Jesus Christ is our example in that He never once performed a non-sacred act. His life was filled with power and prayer! Hopefully, we desire the same, but to get there we need to realize and practice every day that there is no non-sacred act. For instance, mowing the yard, washing the dishes, cleaning a garage, getting some exercise, organizing a shelf, writing a report, and hundreds more such secular acts should not rob us of intimate fellowship and prayer with God but should enrich it. Of course, that might mean that we have to unplug ourselves partially from the technology that intrudes into our thoughts, that seemingly magnifies our importance, that fills our time with meaninglessness, that stifles us from hearing God's voice, and that undermines the sweet fellowship with Him that He desires for all His children.

REFLECT AND APPLY

1. As Tozer writes in the final paragraph, we should meditate "upon this truth," [i.e., "living to the glory of God, actually and determinedly" in all we do] by talking it over with God often in our prayers, by recalling it to our minds frequently." Do this for a day, then a week, and finally a month. We need to replace this sacred-secular perspective with the divine perspective that our daily labors can be performed as acts of worship acceptable to God. It will take much "reverent prayer to escape completely from the sacred-secular psychology." Second, as God effects the escape, note the changes in your prayer life and your awareness of things that happen around you that God brings to your attention to pray about as well.

2. "The Lord Jesus Christ Himself is our perfect example, and He knew no divided life." Tozer notes that Jesus "lived in that body here among men and never once performed a non-sacred act." As believers, we need to ask ourselves under the searching of the Holy Spirit, do we live divided lives? Is the sacred act of praying separate from the secular activities of life? If separated, we will not respond to situations of stress, pain, difficulty, and more with spontaneous prayer in our heart and mind. Reflect on your past forty-eight hours as to whether there was separation or not between sacred and secular. Be honest!

3. Self-deception can hinder us from truly seeing the separation between the sacred and secular that has slowly occurred in our life and its impact on

our prayer life. If struggling for insight in living to the glory of God, seek out a mature believer to encourage you in this journey.

4. If access to such a believer is not available, consider the following example and your response: You are walking through a parking lot and notice a piece of paper. Since it looks like one that you have been carrying in your pocket, you pick it up to be sure. It is a draft of a letter to someone's parole officer. The writer of the letter evidently had been arrested for drug possession and sent to the jail, but now, years later, his/her life has turned around. The individual, now married, is seeking an end to the parole.

Would you respond with indifference and throw the piece of paper down immediately? Would you respond with contempt for the person? Would you say, "Except for the grace of God, I would be there too"? Or would you respond with empathy as you pray for this individual's plight, salvation, and future? One might even write on the note "I'm praying for you" and place it by the truck it was near. This is a secular event that can and should become sacred. The two merge easily for the individual who does all to the glory of God. There are many such events in each of our days to bless and pray!

3

THE SACRAMENT OF LIVING: PART 2

This is not quite all regarding the sacred versus the secular. Long-held habits do not die easily. It will take intelligent thought and a great deal of reverent prayer to escape completely from the sacred-secular psychology.

For instance, it may be difficult for the average Christian to get hold of the idea that his daily labors can be performed as acts of worship acceptable to God by Jesus Christ. The old antithesis will crop up in the back of his head sometimes to disturb his peace of mind. Nor will that old serpent, the devil, take all this lying down. He will be there in the car or at the desk or in the field to remind the Christian that he is giving the better part of his day to the things of this world and allotting to his religious duties only a trifling portion of his time. And unless great care is taken, this will create confusion and bring discouragement and heaviness of heart.

We can meet this successfully only by the exercise of an aggressive faith. We must offer all our acts to God and believe that He accepts them. Then hold firmly to that position and keep insisting that every act of every hour of the day and night be included in the transaction. Keep reminding God in our times of private prayer that we mean every act for His glory; then supplement those times by a thousand thought-prayers as we go about the job of living. Let us practice the fine art of making every work a priestly ministration. Let us believe that God is in all our simple deeds and learn to find Him there.

A concomitant of the error that we have been discussing is the sacred-secular antithesis as applied to places. It is little short of astonishing that we can read the New Testament and still believe in the inherent sacredness of some places. This error is so widespread that one feels all alone when he tries to combat it. It has acted as a kind of dye to color the thinking of religious persons and has colored the eyes as well so that it is all but impossible to detect its fallacy. In the face of every New Testament teaching to the contrary, it has been said and sung throughout the centuries and accepted as a part of the Christian message, that which it most surely is not. Only the Quakers, so far as my knowledge goes, have had the perception to see the error and the courage to expose it.

Here are the facts as I see them. For four hundred years Israel had dwelt in Egypt, surrounded by the crassest idolatry. By the hand of Moses they were brought out at last and started toward the land of promise. The very idea of holiness had been lost to them. To correct this, God began at the bottom. He localized Himself in the cloud and fire, and later when the tabernacle had been built, He dwelt in fiery manifestation in the Holy of

Holies. By innumerable distinctions God taught Israel the difference between holy and unholy. There were holy days, holy vessels, holy garments. There were washings, sacrifices, offerings of many kinds. By these means, Israel learned that *God is holy.* It was this that He was teaching them, not the holiness of things or places. The holiness of Jehovah was the lesson they must learn.

Then came the great day when Christ appeared. Immediately He began to say, "Ye have heard that it was said of them of old time . . . But I say unto you" (Matt. 5:21–22). The Old Testament schooling was over. When Christ died on the cross, the veil of the temple was rent from top to bottom. The Holy of Holies was opened to everyone who would enter in faith. Christ's words were remembered, "The hour cometh, when ye shall neither in this mountain, nor yet at Jerusalem, worship the Father . . . . But the hour cometh, and now is, when the true worshippers shall worship the Father in spirit and in truth: for the Father seeketh such to worship him. God is a Spirit: and they that worship him must worship him in spirit and in truth" (John 4:21, 23 –24).

Shortly after, Paul took up the cry of liberty and declared all meats clean, every day holy, all places sacred, and every act acceptable to God. The sacredness of times and places, a half-light necessary to the education of the race, passed away before the full sun of spiritual worship.

The essential spirituality of worship remained the possession of the church until it was slowly lost with the passing of the years. Then the natural *legality* of the fallen hearts of men began to introduce the old distinctions. The church came to observe again days and seasons and times. Certain places were chosen and marked out as holy in a special sense. Differences were observed between one and another day or place or person. The "sacraments" were first two, then three, then four, until with the triumph of Romanism they were fixed at seven.

In all charity, and with no desire to reflect unkindly upon any Christian, however misled, I would point out that the Roman Catholic church represents today the sacred-secular heresy carried to its logical conclusion. Its deadliest effect is the complete cleavage it introduces between religion and life. Its teachers attempt to avoid this snare by many footnotes and multitudinous explanations, but the mind's instinct for logic is too strong. In practical living the cleavage is a fact.

From this bondage Reformers and Puritans and mystics have labored to free us. Today, the trend in conservative circles is back toward that bondage again. It is said that a horse, after it has been led out of a burning building, will sometimes, by a strange obstinacy, break loose from its rescuer and dash back into the building again to perish in the flame. By some such stubborn tendency toward error, fundamentalism in our day is moving back toward spiritual slavery. The observation of days and times is becoming more and more prominent among us. "Lent" and "holy week" and "good" Friday are words heard more and more frequently upon the lips of gospel Christians. We do not know when we are well off.

In order that I may be understood and not be misunderstood, I would throw into relief the practical implications of the teaching for which I have been arguing, i.e., the sacramental quality of everyday living. Over against its positive meanings, I should like to point out a few things it does not mean.

It does not mean, for instance, that everything we do is of

equal importance with everything else we do or may do. One act of a good man's life may differ widely from another in importance. Paul's sewing of tents was not equal to his writing of an epistle to the Romans, but both were accepted of God and both were true acts of worship. Certainly it is more important to lead a soul to Christ than to plant a garden, but the planting of the garden *can* be as holy an act as the winning of a soul. . . .

The "layman" need never think of his humbler task as being inferior to that of his minister. Let every man abide in the calling wherein he is called, and his work will be as sacred as the work of the ministry. It is not what a man does that determines whether his work is sacred or secular, it is why he does it. The motive is everything. Let a man sanctify the Lord God in his heart and he can thereafter do no common act. All he does is good and acceptable to God through Jesus Christ. For such a man, living itself will be a priestly ministration. As he performs his never-so-simple task, he will hear the voice of the seraphim saying, "Holy, holy, holy, is the Lord of hosts: the whole earth is full of his glory" (Isa. 6:3).

From *The Pursuit of God*
(1948; repr., Chicago: Moody, 2015)

EXPLORING WITH TOZER

Part 2 of "The Sacrament of Living" is a continuation of the conflict between sacred and secular but with a focus on specifics. For instance, the separation between secular and sacred tends to be a long-held habit of believers, and such habit breaking needs to be recognized as a spiritual battle. This battle will require aggressive faith in God and much prayer, but the outworkings of such must be continuous throughout each day. For sure, there will be lapses or failures in this struggle, but we press on clinging even more to our Savior. In addition, Tozer does note that this struggle for holiness in all we do was a recurrent problem in the history of Israel, during the early church, and in the church since that time. It is a reality that we cannot ignore, but in Christ and Christ alone there is victory!

REFLECT AND APPLY

1. Tozer rightly notes that success in this struggle between sacred and secular is possible only by the exercise of an aggressive faith. We must offer all our acts to God and believe that He accepts them. Then hold firmly to that position and keep insisting that every act of every hour of the day and night be included in the transaction. Keep reminding God in our times of private prayer that we mean every act for His glory; then supplement those times by a thousand thought-prayers as we go about the job of living. Let us practice the fine art of making every work a priestly ministration.

    Tozer points to four steps in this process: (1) aggressive faith in God, (2) a surrender of all of our acts to Him, (3) private prayer and (4) thousands of thought-prayers. Is your private prayer squeezed by the world? How do you protect that time?

2. Private prayer and thousands of thought-prayers must both be present in the life of the believer that is trying to break away from the sacred-secular dichotomy. Why?

3. It is usually easier to evaluate private prayer since it is typically delegated to a certain time or times of a day, but thought-prayers have more freedom about them since they are at the total prompting of the Holy Spirit at a moment. What significant thought-prayers have you had in the past twenty-four hours?

4. The Reformers, Puritans and mystics have labored to free us from the bondage of this sacred-secular heresy. "Today, the trend in conservative circles is back toward that bondage again." List some man-ifestations of this bondage that you have seen in your life and church and how it has affected your prayer life.

5. Finally, "Let every man abide in the calling wherein he is called and his work will be as sacred as the work of the ministry. It is not what a man does that determines whether his work is sacred or secular; it is why he does it. The motive is every-thing." Proverbs 16:2 says: "All the ways of a man are clean in his own sight, but the Lord weighs the motives." Reflect on your motives for your calling! Ponder your motives for your prayers! If your mo-tives are not right, what does one do next?

4

TO BE RIGHT, WE
MUST THINK RIGHT

What we think about when we are free to think about whatever we will—that is what we are or will soon become.

The Bible has a great deal to say about our thoughts; current evangelicalism has practically nothing to say about them. The reason the Bible says so much is that our thoughts are so vitally important to us; the reason evangelicalism says so little is that we are overreacting from the "thought" cults, such as New Thought, Unity, Christian Science, and the like. These cults make our thoughts to be very nearly everything, and we counter by making them very nearly nothing. Both positions are wrong.

Our voluntary thoughts not only reveal what we are; they predict what we will become. Except for that conduct which springs from our basic natural instincts, all conscious behavior is preceded by and arises out of our thoughts. The will can become a servant of the thoughts, and to a large degree even our emotions follow our thinking. "The more I think about it the madder I get" is the way the average man states it, and in so doing not only reports accurately on his own mental processes but pays as well an unconscious tribute to the power of thought. Thinking stirs feeling and feeling triggers action. That is the way we are made and we may as well accept it.

The Psalms and Prophets contain numerous references to the power of right thinking to raise religious feeling and incite us to right conduct. "I thought on my ways, and turned my feet unto thy testimonies" (Ps. 119:59). "While I was musing the fire burned: then spake I with my tongue" (Ps. 39:3). Over and over the Old Testament writers exhort us to get quiet and think about high and holy things as a preliminary to amendment of life or a good deed or a courageous act.

The Old Testament is not alone in its respect for the God-given power of human thought. Christ taught that men defile themselves by evil thinking and even went so far as to equate a thought with an act: "Whosoever looketh on a woman to lust after her hath committed adultery with her already in his heart" (Matt. 5:28). Paul recited a list of shining virtues and commanded, "Think on these things" (Phil. 4:8).

These quotations are but four out of hundreds that could be cited from the Scriptures. Thinking about God and holy things creates a moral climate favorable to the growth of faith and love and humility and reverence. We cannot by thinking regenerate our hearts, nor take our sins away nor change the leopard's spots. Neither can we by thinking add one cubit to our stature or make evil good or darkness light. So to teach is to misrepresent a scriptural truth and to use it to our own undoing. But we can by Spirit-inspired thinking help to make our minds pure sanctuaries in which God will be pleased to dwell.

I referred in a previous paragraph to "our voluntary thoughts," and I used the words advisedly. In our journey through this evil and hostile world, many thoughts will be forced upon us which we do not like and for which we have no moral sympathy. The necessity to make a living may compel us for days on end to entertain thoughts in no sense elevating. Ordinary awareness of the doings of our fellow men will bring thoughts repugnant to our Christian soul. These need affect us but little. For them we are not responsible, and they may pass through our minds like a bird through the air, without leaving a trace. They have no lasting effect upon us because they are not our own. They are unwelcome intruders for which we have no love and which we get rid of as quickly as possible.

Anyone who wishes to check on his true spiritual condition may do so by noting what his voluntary thoughts have been over the last hours or days. What has he thought about when free to think of what he pleased? Toward what has his inner heart turned when it was free to turn where it would? When the bird of thought was let go did it fly out like the raven to settle upon floating carcasses, or did it like the dove circle and return again to the ark of God? Such a test is easy to run, and if we are honest with ourselves we can discover not only what we are but also what we are going to become. We'll soon be the sum of our voluntary thoughts.

While our thoughts stir our feelings, and thus strongly influence our wills, it is yet true that the will can be and should be master of our thoughts. Every normal person can determine what he will think about. Of course the troubled or tempted man may find his thoughts somewhat difficult to control and even while he is concentrating upon a worthy object, wild and fugitive thoughts may play over his mind like heat lightning on a summer evening. These are likely to be more bothersome than harmful and in the long run do not make much difference one way or another.

The best way to control our thoughts is to offer the mind to God in complete surrender. The Holy Spirit will accept it and take control of it immediately. Then it will be relatively easy to think on spiritual things, especially if we train our thought by long periods of daily prayer. Long practice in the art of mental prayer (that is, talking to God inwardly as we work or travel) will help to form the habit of holy thought.

From *Born After Midnight*
(1959; repr., Chicago: Moody, 2015)

EXPLORING WITH TOZER

Outwardly, this selection seems very similar to the previous two chapters on the sacred-secular dilemma, but in reality it looks at the core of the problem: right thinking leads to right doing. The right doing we are focused on is right praying, and right thinking begins with hiding God's Word not only in our hearts and minds but allowing it to renew our minds in all spheres of life, the sacred and the secular. Romans 12:1–2 captures this process:

Therefore I urge you, brethren, by the mercies of God, to present your bodies a living and holy sacrifice, acceptable to God, which is your spiritual service of worship. And do not be conformed to this world, but be transformed by the renewing of your mind, so that you may prove what the will of God is, that which is good and acceptable and perfect.

Of course, this process takes time, a complete surrender of the mind to God, and discipline in the power of the Holy Spirit to become a reality. As our God transforms our mind and hearts, then our prayer life will also experience that transformation as we seek and pray for the will of God in all.

Tozer mentions two kinds of thought: forced and voluntary. The forced thoughts he described as those "which we do not like and for which we have no moral sympathy" and which are "repugnant to our Christian soul." These are intruders that pass through and leave no trace. But what about the forced thoughts that are distortions, lies, half-truths, and dangerous subtleties that undermine our faith in God like the serpent did to Eve in the garden of Eden (Gen. 3:1–5)? If these kinds of thoughts are not screened through the Word of God or, better yet, exposed to the light of God's Word, the end result will be defective prayer, less prayer, and eventually no prayer. "Satan is waging war against God—and the stakes are high: the control of the minds of Christians."[1]

Tozer uses the "voluntary thoughts" over the last hours or days as the litmus test of our true spiritual condition. The leanings of those voluntary thoughts reveal the directions of the inner heart.

Proverbs 23:7 says, "For as he thinks within himself ([or literally reckons in his soul]), so he is." Thus, those thoughts or reckonings in the soul will reveal the total essence of a man or woman and their desire to please the Father in prayer.

REFLECT AND APPLY

1. Take an inventory of your voluntary thoughts over the past week. Have those thoughts gravitated toward the things of God and prayer or toward daily activities or personal goals? Take one piece of paper and jot down the tendencies of your thoughts in two columns: God or elsewhere. On the other side of the paper, jot down the tendencies of your prayers this past week: God's kingdom or your kingdom. Assess the correlation of the two results. What must you do next?

2. Tozer talks of training our thoughts by long periods of daily prayer. How do we do that in our busy, fast-paced, multitasking, technology-dominated world or culture? Try some changes in your lifestyle for a week to see if your time for prayer and your tendency to pray is improved.

3. "Long practice in the art of mental prayer (that is talking to God inwardly as we work or travel) will help to form the habit of holy thought." Try this for a day, then a week, and finally a month. Assess this experiment or better yet evaluate it with a mentor or another believer. Accountability in this experiment will go a long way to making it successful in the eyes of God.

4. As you try to see God have more control over your voluntary thoughts, how has it affected your response to temptation, to confession of sin, to daily worship, to the needs of others, and to the plight of our nation?

5

PRAYER: NO SUBSTITUTE FOR OBEDIENCE

Have you noticed how much praying for revival has been going on of late—and how little revival has resulted?

Considering the volume of prayer that is ascending these days, rivers of revival should be flowing in blessing throughout the land. That no such results are in evidence should not discourage us; rather it should stir us to find out why our prayers are not answered.

Everything has its proper cause in the kingdom of God as well as in the natural world. The reason for God's obvious refusal to send revival may lie deep, but surely not too deep to discover.

I believe our problem is that we have been trying to substitute praying for obeying; and it simply will not work.

A church, for instance, follows its traditions without much thought about whether they are scriptural or not. Or it surrenders to pressure from public opinion and falls in with popular trends which carry it far from the New Testament pattern. Then the leaders notice a lack of spiritual power among the people and become concerned about it. What to do? How can they achieve that revitalization of spirit they need so badly? How can they bring down refreshing showers to quicken their fainting souls?

The answer is all ready for them. The books tell them how—pray! The passing evangelist confirms what the books have said—pray! The word is echoed back and forth, growing in volume until it becomes a roar—pray! So the pastor calls his people to prayer. Days and nights are spent begging God to be merciful and send revival upon His people. The tide of feeling runs high and it looks for a while as if the revival might be on the way. But it fails to arrive and the zeal for prayer begins to flag. Soon the church is back where it was before, and a numb discouragement settles over everyone. What has gone wrong?

Simply this: Neither the leaders nor the people have made any effort to obey the Word of God. They felt that their only weakness was failure to pray, when actually in a score of ways they were falling short in the vital matter of obedience. "To obey is better than sacrifice" (1 Sam. 15:22). Prayer is never an acceptable substitute for obedience. The sovereign Lord accepts no offering from His creatures that is not accompanied by obedience. To pray for revival while ignoring or actually flouting the plain precept laid down in the Scriptures is to waste a lot of words and get nothing for our trouble.

It has been overlooked in recent times that the faith of Christ is an absolute arbiter. It preempts the whole redeemed personality and seizes upon the individual to the exclusion of all other claims. Or more accurately, it makes every legitimate claim on the Christian's life conditional, and without hesitation decides the place each claim shall have in the total scheme. The act of committal to Christ in salvation releases the believing man from the penalty of sin, but it does not release him from the obligation to obey the words of Christ. Rather it brings him under the joyous necessity to obey.

Look at the epistles of the New Testament and notice how largely they are given over to what is erroneously called "hortatory," or exhorting, matters. By dividing the epistles into "doctrinal" and "hortatory" passages, we have relieved ourselves of any necessity to obey the advisory sections. The doctrinal passages require from us nothing except that we believe them. The so-called hortatory passages are harmless enough, for the very word *hortatory* declares them to be words of advice and encouragement rather than commandments to be obeyed. This is a palpable error.

The exhortations in the epistles are to be understood as apostolic injunctions carrying the weight of mandatory charges from the Head of the church, Christ Himself. They are intended to be obeyed, not weighed as bits of good advice which we are at liberty to accept or reject as we will.

If we would have God's blessing upon us, we must begin to obey. Prayer will become effective when we stop using it as a substitute for obedience. God will not accept praying in lieu of obeying. We only deceive ourselves when we try to make the substitution.

From *Of God and Men*
(1960; repr., Chicago: Moody, 2015)

EXPLORING WITH TOZER

The words of Samuel the prophet to Saul the first king of Israel "to obey is better than sacrifice" (1 Sam. 15:22) are in the context of Saul offering the Lord the best of the sheep or of the bounty from the Amalekites instead of the ultimate best thing of just obeying the Lord's Word. This is a struggle all believers have in focusing on the good instead of the ultimate best. Tozer makes that connection with prayer and obedience. For more clarity on these thoughts, look at the Lord's words to Jeremiah:

> For they have turned their back to Me, and not their face; but in the time of their trouble they will say, "Arise and save us." (2:27)

> I will show them My back and not My face in the day of their calamity. (18:17)

> And they have turned their back to Me and not their face; though I taught them, teaching again and again, they would not listen and receive instruction. (32:33)

These words to Jeremiah rightly depict a walk of disobedience to the Lord ("their back to Me"), not a face that prays when troubles or difficult times come. Prayer to the Lord must be grounded in the roots of a life of obedience to the Lord in the power of the Holy Spirit. As a result, God reciprocates to the disobedient with showing His back and not His face, i.e., their prayers are not answered. This is the point that Tozer has made with so much prayer for revival and no or so few results. There must be a search or an assessment for the reason why our prayers are not answered. This honest assessment must be made by the individual believer and by the corporate body of believers. Without it, we will go backward and not forward (Jer. 7:24) in our walk with Christ and in our prayer life.

REFLECT AND APPLY

1. Tozer notes that during his span of ministry (1919 to 1963), there was much praying for revival, during a time of two world wars and the Great Depression. In many ways, the times are not much better now. Is your church praying for a revival? Are you praying likewise? Assess your prayers for revival both locally and nationally. Assess your obedience to the Lord's words as well over the past thirty days. Is there a dependence between the two streams of your prayer for revival and your obedience to the Lord? What should you do?

2. Why is praying for revival so much easier to do than obeying God's Word? This is a critical honest assessment that every believer must make before their prayer life can be characterized by power from on high.

3. Tozer talks about zeal for prayer lagging, numb discouragement for prayer, and deceived people when we try to substitute prayer for obedience. Get alone with the Lord, and ask Him to restore your zeal for daily obedience and a prayer life that responds to the daily challenges and opportunities.

4. Finally, be careful that you do not get in a legalistic bondage with prayer and obedience. It is easy to think that the more one obeys the more God owes the person in prayer. When the believer is obedient to the Lord, he develops the mind of Christ and prays more about what God lays before him to pray about. There is not a legalistic nature about it but a freedom to be about the Father's business and to be a blessing to those in our sphere of influence. Ask the Spirit of God to search you and to purge you of such ungodly perspectives!

6

THE IMPORTANCE OF PRAYER IN GOD'S ETERNAL WORK

The biblical teaching that God's work through the church can be accomplished only by the energizing of the Holy Spirit is very hard for us humans to accept. It is a fact that frustrates our carnal desire for honor and praise, for glory and recognition.

Basically, God has been very kind and tender toward us. But there is no way in which He can compromise with our human pride and carnality. That is why His Word bears down so hard on "proud flesh," insisting that we understand and confess that no human gifts, no human talents can accomplish the ultimate and eternal work of God.

The glory can belong only to God. If we take the glory, God is being frustrated in the church.

Consider, then, what Jesus Christ actually did. He gave special gifts "for the perfecting of the saints, for the work of the ministry, for the edifying of the body of Christ" (Eph. 4:12). The ministry that the saints are to do—and the reference is not just to ordained ministers as we know them—will bring about the building up of the Body of Christ "till we all come in the unity of the faith, and of the knowledge of the Son of God, unto a perfect man, unto the measure of the stature of the fulness of Christ" (4:13).

A second important requirement if the believing church is to be used in God's eternal work is prayer. This matter of prayer really bears on the great privileges of the common people, the children of God. No matter what our stature or status, we have the authority in the family of God to pray the prayer of faith. The prayer of faith engages the heart of God, meeting God's conditions of spiritual life and victory.

Our consideration of the power and efficacy of prayer enters into the question of why we are part of a Christian congregation and what that congregation is striving to be and do. We have to consider whether we are just going around and around—like a religious merry-go-round. Are we simply holding on to the painted mane of the painted horse, repeating a trip of very insignificant circles to a pleasing musical accompaniment?

Some may think the path of the religious carousel is a kind of progress, but the family of God knows better. We are among those who believe in something more than holding religious services in the same old weekly groove. We believe that in an assembly of redeemed believers there should be marvelous answers to prayer.

We believe that God hears and actually answers our praying in the Spirit. One miraculous answer to prayer within a congregation will do more to lift, encourage and solidify the people of God than almost any other thing. Answers to our prayers will lift up the hands that hang down in discouragement and strengthen the feeble spiritual knees.

All of the advertising we can do will never equal the interest and participation in the things of God resulting from the gracious answers to the prayers of faith generated by the Holy Spirit.

Actually, it will be such prayer and the meeting of God's conditions that bring us to the third requirement if God is to fulfill His ordained accomplishments through the church. I speak of the Christian's dependence on the Holy Spirit and our willingness to exercise the Spirit's gifts.

From *Tragedy in the Church*
(1990; repr., Camp Hill, PA: WingSpread, 2010)

EXPLORING WITH TOZER

Tozer continually notes that "the biblical teaching that God's work through the church can be accomplished only by the energizing of the Holy Spirit is a fact that frustrates our desire for honor and praise, glory and recognition." It is the frailty of our depraved nature to want to take credit for our gifts, our talents, the work that God has sovereignly given each of us to do, and the success (never the failure) of that divine labor. However, the glory of it all (success or failure) belongs only to God. Some may say that the failure is all ours, but is it not possible that God has allowed the failure to break us of self-sufficiency so that He gets the glory for moving us to be more dependent upon Him?

Likewise, the Holy Spirit must energize our prayer life. We cannot pray with the discipline of the flesh and be heard. We cannot boast of our answers to prayer. We cannot be people of prayer to be seen by people. No, it must be all of God! The Holy Spirit initiates the prayer of the saint as we quietly hear His voice, gives the believer promises to cling to in this prayer journey, and empowers the believer to persevere in prayer. The Spirit also enables the believer to give God the glory when the answer comes and enriches the believer's life with the Savior as a result of this unbeknown service to others. For sure, God sees it and rewards this Holy Spirit-driven obedience in His time!

REFLECT AND APPLY

1. Tozer mentions that "in an assembly of redeemed believers there should be marvelous answers to prayer." Are you aware of such answered prayers in your church? What has been your response? Are you aware of such answered prayers in your life? What was your response then and now?

2. It is very easy to be trapped in a religious merry-go-round, "simply holding on to the painted mane of the painted horse, repeating a trip of very insignificant circles to a pleasing musical accompaniment." The Psalmist writes, "Be still ["cease striving" NASB] and know that I am God" (Ps. 46:10). Let God search your heart to see if you are on such a merry-go-round in your church, in your

own walk with Him, and most importantly in your prayer life. In light of your assessment, what must be done next?

3. Does one miraculous answer to prayer within your congregation lift, encourage, and solidify the saints in your church more than almost anything? If the answer is yes, what was the miracle? If the answer is no, what conclusions or assessments need to be made quickly? Likewise, consider these same questions for yourself.

4. "All of the advertising we can do will never equal the interest and participation in the things of God resulting from the gracious answers to the prayers of faith generated by the Holy Spirit." Is this the model of today's church? Your church? How do we begin to move back to the biblical model where everything is driven by the Holy Spirit, even our prayer?

BORN AFTER MIDNIGHT

Among revival-minded Christians I have heard the saying, "Revivals are born after midnight."

This is one of those proverbs which, while not quite literally true, yet points to something very true. If we understand the saying to mean that God does not hear our prayer for revival made in the daytime, it is of course not true. If we take it to mean that prayer offered when we are tired and worn-out has greater power than prayer made when we are rested and fresh, again it is not true. God would need to be very austere indeed to require us to turn our prayer into penance, or to enjoy seeing us punish ourselves by intercession. Traces of such ascetical notions are still found among some gospel Christians, and while these brethren are to be commended for their zeal, they are not to be excused for unconsciously attributing to God a streak of sadism unworthy of fallen men.

Yet there is considerable truth in the idea that revivals are born after midnight, for revivals (or any other spiritual gifts and graces) come only to those who want them badly enough. It may be said without qualification that every man is as holy and as full of the Spirit as he wants to be. He may not be as full as he wishes he were, but he is most certainly as full as he wants to be.

Our Lord placed this beyond dispute when He said, "Blessed are they which do hunger and thirst after righteousness: for they shall be filled." Hunger and thirst are physical sensations which, in their acute stages, may become real pain. It has been the experience of countless seekers after God that when their desires became a pain, they were suddenly and wonderfully filled. The problem is not to persuade God to fill us, but to want God sufficiently to permit Him to do so. The average Christian is so cold and so contented with His wretched condition that there is no vacuum of desire into which the blessed Spirit can rush in satisfying fullness.

Occasionally there will appear on the religious scene a man whose unsatisfied spiritual longings become so big and important in his life that they crowd out every other interest. Such a man refuses to be content with the safe and conventional prayers of the frost-bound brethren who "lead in prayer" week after week and year after year in the local assemblies. His yearnings carry him away and often make something of a nuisance out of him. His puzzled fellow Christians shake their heads and look knowingly at each other, but like the blind man who cried after his sight and was rebuked by the disciples, he "cries the more a great deal." And if he has not yet met the conditions or there is something hindering the answer to his prayer, he may pray on into the late hours. Not the hour of night but the state of his heart decides the time of his visitation. For him it may well be that revival comes after midnight.

It is very important, however, that we understand that long prayer vigils, or even strong crying and tears, are not in themselves meritorious acts. Every blessing flows out of the goodness of God as from a fountain. Even those rewards for good works about which certain teachers talk so fulsomely, and which they always set in sharp contrast to the benefits received by grace alone, are at bottom as certainly of grace as is the forgiveness of sin itself. The holiest apostle can claim no more than that he is an unprofitable servant. The very angels exist out of the pure goodness of God. No creature can "earn" anything in the usual meaning of the word. All things are by and of the sovereign goodness of God.

Lady Julian summed it up quaintly when she wrote, "It is more honor to God, and more very delight, that we faithfully pray to Himself of His goodness and cleave thereunto by His grace, and with true understanding, and steadfast by love, than if we took all the means that heart can think. For if we took all those means it is too little, and not full honor to God. But in His goodness is all the whole, and there faileth right nought. . . . For the goodness of God is the highest prayer, and it cometh down to the lowest part of our need."

Yet for all God's goodwill toward us He is unable to grant us our heart's desires till all our desires have been reduced to one. When we have dealt with our carnal ambitions; when we have trodden upon the lion and adder of the flesh, have trampled the dragon of self-love under our feet and have truly reckoned ourselves to have died unto sin, then and only then can God raise us to newness of life and fill us with His blessed Holy Spirit.

It is easy to learn the doctrine of personal revival and victorious living; it is quite another thing to take our cross and plod on to the dark and bitter hill of self-renunciation. Here many are called and few are chosen. For every one that actually crosses over into the Promised Land, there are many who stand for a while and look longingly across the river and then turn sadly back to the comparative safety of the sandy wastes of the old life.

No, there is no merit in late-hour prayers, but it requires a serious mind and a determined heart to pray past the ordinary into the unusual. Most Christians never do. And it is more than possible that the rare soul who presses on into the unusual experience reaches there after midnight.

From *Born after Midnight*
(1959; repr., Chicago: Moody, 2015)

EXPLORING WITH TOZER

Knowingly or unknowingly, most Christians have some serious misconceptions about prayer, specifically as it relates to revival. Long prayer vigils, prayer tainted with strong crying and tears, prayer offered when we are tired and worn-out, late night prayer sessions, and more can have ascetic shadows that are not rooted deeply in God. As Tozer notes, "No creature can 'earn' anything in the usual meaning of the word."

All things are by and of the sovereign goodness of God.

Likewise, Lady Julian addressed this issue by saying "for the goodness of God is the highest prayer, and it comes down to the lowest part of our need."

In truth, "revivals come only to those who want them badly enough," and that tends to be individuals whose heart desires have all been reduced to one, knowing and pleasing Him (Col. 1:10–18) in such a way that Christ might come to have first place in everything. This journey of taking up our cross and plodding "on to the dark and bitter hill of self-renunciation" is impossible without clinging to Christ in the power of the Holy Spirit and moving in the directions His Spirit leads us. Tozer rightly points out that "many are called" for this journey, but many of this many may look back "to the comparative safety of the sandy waste places of the old life." The end result is little fruit, little salt and light influence on our sphere of influence, little power, and a weak or nonexistent prayer life.

REFLECT AND APPLY

1. We each need to ask ourselves what do we want to the utmost. Do we want a comfortable life economically for ourselves and our family? Do we want to see our children do well? Do we want recognition in our job or in the use of our spiritual gifts? This list of "what do we want badly enough?" could go on and on. However, where is our desire for revival for ourselves, our family, our church, our community, our state, and our nation? If we really want revival "badly enough," will not our spiritual longings begin to crowd out every other interest? In addition, will not our gravitation

to safe and conventional prayers be less and less? Consider this fervent prayer for revival by the minor prophet Habakkuk in Habakkuk 3:2: "I have heard the report about You and I fear. O Lord, revive Your work in the midst of the years, in the midst of the years make it known; in wrath remember mercy." Reflect and meditate on this prayer. Make it your prayer!

2. Maybe the essence of wanting revival "badly enough" is found in the following verse: "If My people who are called by My name humble themselves and pray and seek My face and turn from their wicked ways, then I will hear from heaven, will forgive their sin and will heal their land (2 Chronicles 7:14).

    True revival has four conditions: humbling ourselves before God, praying, seeking God's face, and turning from our wicked ways. Of course, meeting these conditions is not possible except under the leading and power of the Holy Spirit; but it will take time. With progress in these conditions, God will hear our prayers, forgive our sin, and heal our land. Thus, "He is unable to grant us our heart's desires till all our desires have been reduced to one." Ask God to search your own heart as to where you are at with these four conditions. Ask Him to help you want His will in your life!

3. "No, there is no merit in late hour prayers, but it requires a serious mind and a determined heart to pray past the ordinary into the unusual. Most Christians never do. And it is more possible that the rare soul who presses on into the unusual experience reaches there after midnight."

Honestly assess where you are in light of this Tozer quote. Serious or lightly committed mentally? Determined or half-hearted? What must you do to be one of these rare souls, who pursues God in prayer?

4. Tozer quotes Lady Julian on the goodness of God and prayer. She noted that "the goodness of God is the highest prayer, and it can come down to the lowest part of our need." Reflect, discuss, and pray about this profound truth!

PRAYING WITHOUT CONDITION

Julian of Norwich at the beginning of her wonderful Christian life addressed a prayer to her Savior and then added the wise words, "And this I ask without any condition."

It was that last sentence that gave power to the rest of her prayer and brought the answer in mighty poured-out floods as the years went by. God could answer her prayer because He did not need to mince matters with her. She did not hedge her prayers around with disclaimers and provisos. She wanted certain things from God at any cost. God, as it were, had only to send her the bill. She would pay any price to get what she conceived to be good for her soul and glorifying to her heavenly Father. That is real praying.

Many of us spoil our prayers by being too "dainty" with the Lord (as some old writer called it). We ask with the tacit understanding that the cost must be reasonable. After all, there is a limit to everything, and we do not want to be fanatical! We want the answer to be something added, not something taken away. We want nothing radical or out of the ordinary, and we want God to accommodate us at our convenience. Thus we attach a rider to every prayer, making it impossible for God to answer it.

In a world like ours, courage is an indispensable virtue. The coward may snivel in his corner, but the brave man takes the prize. And in the kingdom of God, courage is as necessary as it is in the world. The timid soul is as pitiable on his knees as he is in society.

When entering the prayer chamber, we must come filled with faith and armed with courage. Nowhere else in the whole field of religious thought and activity is courage so necessary as in prayer. The successful prayer must be one without condition. We must believe that God is love and that, being love, He cannot harm us but must ever do us good. Then we must throw ourselves before Him and pray with boldness for whatever we know our good and His glory require, and the cost is no object! Whatever He in His love and wisdom would assess against us, we will accept with delight because it pleased Him. Prayers like that cannot go unanswered. The character and reputation of God guarantee their fulfillment.

We should always keep in mind the infinite lovingkindness of God. No one need fear to put his life in His hands. His yoke is easy; His burden is light.

From *We Travel an Appointed Way*
(1988; repr., Camp Hill, PA: WingSpread, 2010)

EXPLORING WITH TOZER

At first glance of this chapter title, one would think that there are no conditions necessary for prayer, such as a clean heart as a result of sins confessed, obedient feet, in faith, with humility, according to God's will as indicated in the Scriptures, abiding in Him and His words in us, and so on. However, the essence of Tozer's words are that we have met these conditions for prayer, and we have asked something of Him.

What we have asked of Him, hopefully, is at the prompting of the Holy Spirit but with conditions attached. For instance, we may be praying for the salvation of a friend, but with the condition that God use someone else while in fact God may want to break us to display His mercies and power in us, "that the life of Jesus also may be manifested in our mortal flesh" (2 Cor. 4:11). Or we may be praying about a legitimate need that God knows we need, but we place stipulations on how that need must be met. In either case, what we have asked of God had at least one condition and that condition hindered God's answer.

The nearest perspective to this thought could be from Ole Hallesby.[1] "Helplessness united with faith produces prayer. Without faith our helplessness would be only a vain cry of distress in the night." Doesn't this helplessness make us more dependent upon Him? We cannot truly be helpless if we continue to lay out a condition for a request of the Father. No condition on our request means we are resting in God's love, grace, and goodness that He will do what is best for all involved and for His glory. When by faith under the leading of the Holy Spirit we acknowledge our helplessness for the request we made to the

Father, we can be sure there will be an answer, but even more that we will come to know Him better.

REFLECT AND APPLY

1. "And this I ask without condition." As Tozer notes, "This sentence gave power to the rest of [Julian's] prayer. . . . God could answer her prayer because He did not need to mince matters with her. She did not hedge her prayers around disclaimers and provisos. She wanted certain things from God at any cost." Truly, that is real praying! Spend some time with God in the very near future to ask Him to search your heart and your ways of praying. To avoid being too introspective, consider the requests that you have made of God in the past thirty days. Ask Him to sensitize your heart and mind in the power of the Holy Spirit to flee from placing such conditions on a request.

2. "Many of us spoil our prayers by being too 'dainty' with the Lord." We are not willing to pay the cost. We want the cost to be reasonable, convenient, ordinary, or mainstream. "We attach a rider to every prayer, making it impossible for God to answer it." List the riders that you have attached to your prayers or requests over the past thirty days on a piece of paper. Burn this piece of paper as a soothing aroma before the Lord and ask Him to change your prayer life.

3. "In the kingdom of God, courage is as necessary as it is in the world. The timid soul is as pitiable on his knees as he is in society. When entering the prayer chamber, we must come filled with faith

and armed with courage." Do you see yourself as armed with courage and filled with faith in your times of prayer? Reflect on how that courage would be displayed.

4. "The successful prayer must be without condition. We must believe that God is love and that, being love, He cannot harm us but must ever do us good. Then we must throw ourselves before Him and pray for boldness for whatever we know our good and His glory require, and the cost is no object." Such praying is nestled in the character and perfect will of God and thus cannot go unanswered. Spend some time, maybe a week or a day on each of the following attributes or perfections of God and on how they affect your prayer life: His self-sufficiency, omniscience, sovereignty, goodness, omnipotence, omnipresence, immutability, wisdom, holiness, love, grace, righteousness, justice, and mercy.

9

THE POWER
OF SILENCE

There are truths that can never be learned except in the noise and confusion of the marketplace or in the tough brutality of combat. The tumult and the shouting teach their own rough lessons. No man is quite a man who has not been to the school of work and war, who has not heard the cry at birth and the sigh at life's parting.

But there is another school where the soul must go to learn its best eternal lessons. It is the school of silence. "Be still and know," said the psalmist, and there is a profound philosophy there, of universal application.

Prayer among evangelical Christians is always in danger of degenerating into a glorified gold rush. Almost every book on prayer deals with the "get" element mainly. How to get things we want from God occupies most of the space. Now, we gladly admit that we may ask for and receive specific gifts and benefits in answer to prayer, but we must never forget that the highest kind of prayer is never the making of requests. Prayer at its holiest moment is the entering into God to a place of such blessed union as makes miracles seem tame and remarkable answers to prayer appear something very far short of wonderful by comparison.

Holy men of soberer and quieter times than ours knew well the power of silence. David said, "I was dumb with silence, I held my peace, even from good; and my sorrow was stirred. My heart was hot within me; while I was musing the fire burned: then spake I with my tongue" (Ps. 39:2–3). There is a tip here for God's modern prophets. The heart seldom gets hot while the mouth is open. A closed mouth before God and a silent heart are indispensable for the reception of certain kinds of truth. No man is qualified to speak who has not first listened.

It might well be a wonderful revelation to some Christians if they were to get completely quiet for a short time, long enough, let us say, to get acquainted with their own souls, and to listen in the silence for the deep voice of the eternal God. The experience, if repeated often enough, would do more to cure our ulcers than all the pills that ever rolled across a desk.

From *The Set of the Sail*

(1986; repr., Camp Hill, PA: WingSpread, 2009)

EXPLORING WITH TOZER

It is highly likely that we do not know the value of silence before God for two reasons. First, we may fail to realize that God is still speaking today and/or that we need solitude with Him to hear that voice. The noise of our fast-paced life, a culture that "destroys men by preventing them from thinking their own thoughts,"[1] wrote Tozer, and our frantic scrambling for significance apart from God all hinder us in hearing His voice. I seriously doubt that most believers could hear the voice of God today as a gentle breeze blowing. Instead, it would require a tornado, or an earthquake, or a fire to get our attention. (See Elijah's encounter with God in 1 Kings 19:11–13.) Even then, we would probably stand around and ask "Why me?" and still not see or hear God in it.

Second, it seems that "religion has accepted the monstrous heresy that noise, size, activity and bluster make a man dear to God."[2] It is time to realize that all of this noise, size, and activity tend to desensitize us to solitude and silence. We need to recall God's words, "Be still and know that I am God" (Ps. 46:10)— and we need God's help in pursuing that stillness, shielded from interferences, demands, and even electronic devices, which are good only if laid before God, in their proper place in our lives. In the midst of great conflict and turmoil—changes, slippage, roarings, and quaking (vv. 2–6)—God says, "Be still, and know that I am God." Tozer interprets this to say that it is "as if He means to tell us that our strength and safety lie not in noise but in silence."[3]

Without this solitude or stillness before God, we cannot cultivate the power of silence. In essence, we saturate our prayers with requests for things or benefits and miss the God of all and the benefactor behind the benefits. Remember that only one Samaritan wanted more than cleansing from leprosy. He wanted to know the Savior. He came back glorifying God, worshiping Him, and giving thanks (Luke 17:11–21). The other nine lepers just had the thing they wanted but the one leper got much more: the Savior and increased faith.

In addition, with diminishing time for solitude and silence before the throne of grace there is a subtle decline in our walk of faith. The less time for solitude before the Lord, the greater the tendency to focus on the "gets" in our prayer. When those "gets" are not received, it is easier for the believer to be deceived that prayer was not worth it. Thus, there is less solitude in the individual believer's life and less asking or less believing that what was asked will be received. The end result is the time before the Lord becomes shorter and shorter. Since the life is filled with activity, we think our prayers must be also.

REFLECT AND APPLY

1. "Prayer among evangelical Christians is always in danger of degenerating into a glorified gold rush." How do we avoid this "get" mentality? How could we redesign our prayer life in such a way that God Himself is more of the focus? Begin with a day per week before the throne of grace with no petitions. Are there other suggestions?

2. "A closed mouth before God and a silent heart are indispensable for the reception of certain kinds of truth. No man is qualified to speak who has not first listened." Why is this silence before God necessary to every believer, as well as to the evangelist, the teacher of God's Word, and those who want to use their spiritual gifts to God's glory?

3. It might be "a wonderful revelation to some Christians if they were to get completely quiet for a short time, long enough, let us say, to get acquainted with their own souls, and to listen in silence for the deep voice of the eternal God." Was there a time in your walk with Christ that you heard the deep voice of the eternal God? If it is not happening now or very infrequently and you want to return to that happening once again, spend some time with a mentor to suggest some steps of grace in the right direction. Season your steps with much prayer and time in the Word of God and with repentance as necessary!

10

DANGERS IN UNANSWERED PRAYER

If unanswered prayer continues in a congregation over an extended period of time, the chill of discouragement will settle over the praying people. If we continue to ask and ask and ask, like petulant children, never expecting to get what we ask for but continuing to whine for it, we will become chilled within our beings.

If we continue in our prayers and never get answers, the lack of results will tend to confirm the natural unbelief of our hearts. Remember this: the human heart by nature is filled with unbelief. Unbelief, not disobedience, was the first sin. While disobedience was the first recorded sin, behind the act of disobedience was the sin of unbelief, else the act of disobedience would not have taken place.

The fact of unanswered prayer will also encourage the idea that religion is unreal, and this idea is held by many people in our day. "Religion is completely subjective," they tell us. "There is nothing real about it."

It is true that there may be nothing tangible to which religion can be referred. If I use the word *lake,* everyone thinks of a large body of water. When I use the word *star,* everyone thinks of a heavenly body. But when I use such words as *faith* and *belief* and *God* and *heaven,* there is not any image of a reality which is known to people and to which their minds immediately refer. To most people, those are just words—like *pixies* and *goblins.* So there is a false idea of unreality in our hearts when we pray and pray and pray and receive no answers.

Perhaps worst of all is the fact that our failures in prayer leave the enemy in possession of the field. The worst part about the failure of a military drive is not the loss of men or the loss of face but the fact that the enemy is left in possession of the field. In the spiritual sense, this is both a tragedy and a disaster. The devil ought to be on the run, always fighting a rear guard action. Instead, this blasphemous enemy smugly and scornfully holds his position, and the people of God let him have it. No wonder the work of the Lord is greatly retarded. Little wonder the work of God stands still!

From *Faith Beyond Reason*
(1990; repr., Camp Hill, PA: WingSpread, 2009)

EXPLORING WITH TOZER

The essence of this short piece on the dangers of unanswered prayer seems to be directed toward the church, but it also has similar implications for the individual believer. For instance, "If unanswered prayer continues in a congregation over an extended period of time, the chill of discouragement will settle over the praying church." Does not the same hold true for the sole believer? It is not only discouragement and unbelief that fill the heart with continual unanswered prayer, but there is a movement away from God and His Word, and self-efforts begin to try to affect the answer ourselves. The end result is less and less biblical praying, and more and more self-effort to help God fulfill our prayer. In addition, a deep deception occurs in our minds and hearts that God has answered "no," "maybe later," or "yes" as we strive for some solution to our original request.

However, is it not possible that much of our unanswered prayer is a result of asking with wrong motives? James 4:3 says "You ask and do not receive because you ask with wrong motives so that you may spend it on your pleasures." Another cause of such unanswered prayer could be sin (either individual or corporate or both) that we have not dealt with before the Lord (Ps. 66:18). That sin could be prolonged sin or recent sin. The Lord makes it plain: "If you abide in Me, and My words abide in you, ask whatever you wish, and it will be done for you" (John 15:7). A walk of obedience to the Word in the power of the Holy Spirit is critical to seeing answered prayer.

It must be said that sometimes unanswered prayer could be a deliberate action from God to see if we would cling to Him when there are no results occurring. Job felt God's absence yet held to Him in Job 23:8–12, which begins in frustration but ends in faith:

> Behold, I go forward but He is not there, and backward, but I cannot perceive Him; when He acts on the left, I cannot behold Him; He turns on the right, I cannot see Him. But He knows the way I take; . . . I have kept His way and not turned aside. I have not departed from the command of His lips; I have treasured the words of His mouth more than my necessary food.

This particular situation usually happens for more mature individual believers and is not what Tozer is addressing. In the natural growth of a church or a believer, there should be answered prayer. The lack of such or an extended time of unanswered prayer should cause a church or a believer to spend some time asking God to search hearts and motives and to expose the impurities. Once God has revealed the sin, may we confess it, accept His forgiveness, and move forward in His will. To fail to do so, will lead to more unanswered prayer, more disappointment, and more unbelief instead of the converse.

REFLECT AND APPLY

1. Tozer notes that "the chill of discouragement will settle over the praying people" when there is unanswered prayer in a congregation over an extended time. The same holds for the individual believer too. How does one assess this situation? Is

it sin in the congregation or in the individual believer's life that is hindering the answer to prayers? Sometimes the sin could be long ago as in the case where Saul and his bloody house put Gibeonites to death who were under God's covenant. The result was a famine for three years until "David sought the presence of the Lord" (2 Sam. 21:1) to find out the problem and God's solution. Or it could be sin that that occurred prior to the unanswered prayer streak. Thus Tozer wrote in *The Warfare of the Spirit,* "The church must examine herself continually to see if she be in the faith; she must engage in severe self-criticism with a cheerful readiness to make amends; she must live in a state of perpetual penitence, seeking God with her whole heart; she must continually check her life and conduct against the Holy Scriptures and bring her life into line with the will of God."[1] These thoughts hold for the individual as well. Ask yourself before the Lord whether this has been your mindset and the direction of your heart prior to this extended time of unanswered prayer.

2. Another possibility for unanswered prayer is that the life of the church or the individual believer has slowly slipped away from holiness and obedience toward more worldly and unscriptural thinking and actions; it may be hard to pinpoint a single event. In that case, we will have to ask God to examine our hearts and our life and to restore us to our first love (Rev. 2:4). He is able to restore us, but we may need others to pinpoint the issues and to jump-start the process of restoration. Pray about this and about who could come alongside and jump-start this restoration.

3. "If we continue in our prayers and never get answers, the lack of results will tend to confirm the natural unbelief of our hearts. Remember this: the human heart by nature is filled with unbelief. Unbelief, not disobedience, was the first sin. While disobedience was the first recorded sin, behind the act of disobedience was the sin of unbelief." The apostle Paul rightly says it: "Test themselves" to see if you are in the faith; examine yourselves (2 Cor. 13:5). We should test whether we are in the faith or whether we are walking by faith. Ask God the Holy Spirit to use the Scriptures to lay bare your heart in these issues of faith and unbelief.[2]

4. Clearly there will be dry times when God does not answer prayer, when our joy fades out, and when the presence of the Lord is felt feebly or not at all. Such times will demand that we exercise faith in a sovereign God. If you have been in such a situation, reflect or discuss the process that God took you through. However, Tozer's focus on unanswered prayer in this specific writing seems not to be this case. Instead, unanswered prayer will feed the thought that religion is unreal and subjective for the not-so-serious believer and the non-believer. The bottom-line is that the cause of Christ is damaged! Alone or with others in a group, list at least three ways the name of Christ is dishonored for the church and another three for the individual believer.

5. "Perhaps worst of all is the fact that our failures in prayer leave the enemy in possession of the field." Tozer notes that this is a tragedy and a disaster since the devil ought to be on the run and on the

defensive. Instead, God's people let the enemy have the field and the work of God is further restrained. As painful as it may be, can you remember a time when your failure in prayer lead to the enemy gaining the field in a life, in a ministry, or in a relationship? What was your response then and what is your response now?

11

WHAT PROFIT IN PRAYER?

The skeptic in the book of Job asked the disdainful question, "What is the Almighty, that we should serve him? And what profit should we have, if we pray unto him?" (Job 21:15).

The whole tone of the remark shows that it is meant to be rhetorical. The doubter, believing the question could have no answer, tossed it off contemptuously and turned away, like Pilate, without waiting for a reply. But we have an answer. God Himself has supplied it, and the universal consensus of the ages has added an *Amen.*

In Hebrews 11 we have a long list of benefits that faith brings to its possessors: justification, deliverance, fruitfulness, endurance, victory over enemies, courage, strength, and even resurrection from the dead. And everything that is attributed to faith might with equal truth be attributed to prayer, for faith and true prayer are like two sides of the same coin. They are inseparable.

Men may, and often do, pray without faith (though this is

not true prayer), but it is not thinkable that men should have faith and not pray. The biblical formula is "The prayer of faith." Prayer and faith are here bound together by the little preposition *of,* and what God hath joined together, let not man put asunder. Faith is only genuine as it eventuates into prayer.

When Tennyson wrote, "More things are wrought by prayer than this world dreams of," he probably uttered a truth of vaster significance than even he understood. While it is not always possible to trace an act of God to its prayer-cause, it is yet safe to say that prayer is in back of everything that God does for the sons of men here upon earth. One would gather as much from a simple reading of the Scriptures.

What profit is there in prayer? "Much every way." Whatever God can do faith can do, and whatever faith can do prayer can do when it is offered in faith. An invitation to prayer is, therefore, an invitation to omnipotence, for prayer engages the omnipotent God and brings Him into our human affairs. Nothing is impossible to the man who prays in faith, just as nothing is impossible with God. This generation has yet to prove all that prayer can do for believing men and women.

It was a saying of George Mueller that faith grows with use. If we would have great faith we must begin to use the little faith we already have. Put it to work by reverent and faithful praying, and it will grow and become stronger day by day. Dare today to trust God for something small and ordinary, and next week or next year you may be able to trust Him for answers bordering on the miraculous. Everyone has some faith, said Mueller; the difference among us is one of degree only, and the man of small faith may be simply the one who has not dared to exercise the little faith he has.

According to the Bible, we have because we ask, or we have not because we ask not. It does not take much wisdom to discover our next move. Is it not to pray, and pray again and again till the answer comes? God waits to be invited to display His power in behalf of His people. The world situation is such that nothing less than God can straighten it out. Let us not fail the world and disappoint God by failing to pray.

From *The Set of the Sail*

(1986; repr., Camp Hill, PA: WingSpread, 2009).

EXPLORING WITH TOZER

To understand the essence of Job's comments to Zophar from Job 21:15, "What is the Almighty, that we should serve him? and what profit should we have, if we pray unto him?" we first need to understand Job's three so-called friends. Bildad was a superficial person, who believed everything can be explained simply in terms of two kinds of men, the blameless and the secretly wicked. Furthermore, his words reflect that these two kinds of men are the same outwardly, but God distinguishes between them by prospering the first and destroying the second. The other two friends, Zophar and Eliphaz, are aptly described by Anderson in the following way:

It is worth pointing out, as a sign of the narrowness of Zophar's beliefs, that his speech (in Job 20) contains no hint that the wicked might repent, make amends and regain the favour of God. Zophar has no compassion and his god has no mercy. By contrast Eliphaz is more humane and evangelical. And Zophar is at heart as much a materialist as the wicked man he condemns. He sees the carrying off of "possessions" (verse 28) as a judgment. The loss of fellowship with God, in this life or after it, does not strike him as a far worse fate.[1]

Job's response to Zophar, the materialist, is that people invested in possessions, things, stuff, and the glory of this world will not see any profit in prayer. Likewise, the nonbeliever or even the materialistic believer today will see little value in prayer.

On the other hand, the upright should see the profit in prayer to God; "the prayer of the upright is his delight" (Prov. 15:8b). There is profit to God in that prayer honors and pleases Him when offered in faith. Secondarily, there is gain for the believer; as his faith in God is increased, his relationship with God becomes stronger, and as his zeal for telling others about what God has done for him cannot be quenched. Tozer rightly connects faith and prayer in this selection. And can it be that we should all ask ourselves is there any profit in not praying?

REFLECT AND APPLY

1. "Men, may, and many do, pray without faith (though this is not true prayer), but it is not thinkable that men should have faith and not pray. The

biblical formula is 'The prayer of faith.' Prayer and faith are here bound together by the little preposition *of*, and what God hath joined together, let not man put asunder. Faith is only genuine as it eventuates into prayer." Consider before the Lord how much of your prayer lately has been vain repetition, or just wishing for things to be a certain way. We must put off the old self and "put on the new self who is being renewed to a true knowledge according to the image of the One who created him" (Col. 3:9–10). That is all by faith! Thus, *our prayer life is a true barometer of our Christian walk*. Reflect on this statement.

2. "While it is not always possible to trace an act of God to its prayer-cause, it is yet safe to say that prayer is back of everything that God does for the sons of men here upon earth." Recall some occasions where your prayers were critical for the miracle that God did. On the other hand, recall some occasions where prayers were made for you and the miraculous answers that came. Each situation should be a common experience in the Christian life, but the lack of such shows weakness in our faith and dims our light to a lost world. Where does one begin to reclaim the lost territory of these experiences?

3. "What profit is there in prayer? 'Much every way.' Whatever God can do faith can do, and whatever faith can do prayer can do when it is offered in faith. An invitation to prayer is, therefore, an invitation to omnipotence, for prayer engages the omnipotent God and brings Him into our human affairs." Is it possible that we don't pray this way of

bringing the omnipotent One into our affairs because we cannot control the results and the timing of those results? Or is it that we don't know the promises of Scripture and the faithful God behind those promises? If serious about prayer and the profit that there is in it, seek out more mature believers who could mentor you in prayer. For the coming week, jot down the profits of prayer that you have seen; and ask God to open your eyes to see the eternal or heavenly profits.

4. "It was a saying of George Mueller that faith grows with use. If we would have great faith, we must begin to use the little faith we already have." Start today! Begin to trust God for small and ordinary things this week, other things a month or two down the road, and some later this year or next. Keep a prayer journal, but also ask God to etch the answers on your heart and mind to share with others to encourage them and to draw them to Christ. After six months, contemplate again the profit in prayer!

THREE WAYS
TO GET WHAT
WE WANT

The word *wish* in its modern sense has little or no place in the Christian's vocabulary. The word occurs rarely in the Bible, and when it does it seldom means more than to will or desire.

It is hard to conceive of anything more completely futile than wishing. It is significant that wishing is done mostly by children and superstitious people. However sweet and innocent it may appear to see a child going through his little ritual of wishing, it can become something far from harmless when carried over into adult life. And even the child should be taught very early that wishing gets him nowhere.

The evil of the empty wish lies in the fact that the wisher is not adjusted to the will of God. He allows his desires to play over things that are entirely out of God's will for him and dreams of possessing what he well knows he should not have. Five minutes of this futile dreaming and he has lost the fine edge off his spiritual life. Should the act ripen into a habit, his Christian life may be seriously injured. The man soon comes to substitute mere longing for hard work, and unless he corrects his fault sharply, he will degenerate into a spineless dreamer of empty dreams.

Every desire should be brought to the test of God's will. If the desire is out of the will of God, it should be instantly dismissed as unworthy of us. To continue to long for something that is plainly out of the will of God for us is to prove how unreal our consecration actually is.

If, however, the desired object is legitimate and innocent, then there are three possible ways by which it may be obtained: one is to work for it, another is to pray for it, and a third is to work and pray for it. These are clear methods by which God gives His good gifts to His people. They are not to be confused with each other and may be distinguished in practical living.

Some things are altogether out of the sphere of possibility for us, and yet altogether within God's gracious will for us. What to do? Prayer is the immediate answer. God has planned that we should go to Him for impossibilities when those impossibilities are a part of His eternal will for our highest good. Under such circumstances we should press our petitions upon Him with all the boldness and ardor of an obedient and trusting child. God loves such praying and has given every reason for us to believe that He will hear our prayer and in due time send the answer.

Other things can be had by the simple expedient of work. It is useless to ask God for something we could obtain with a bit of effort properly directed. No instructed Christian will waste his time praying for things that are within his own power to obtain.

To do so is to deceive ourselves and make a farce of the whole concept of prayer. If work will get it for us, then work it is or we can go without it. God will not contribute to our delinquency by supplying us with gifts which we could get for ourselves but have done nothing to obtain.

But there is a third category consisting of desired objects that work alone can never secure. They lie far enough out of our reach that it will take something supernatural to get them for us, yet near enough that we must labor to obtain them. This adds up to *work and prayer,* and it will probably be found that the greatest majority of desired objects and objectives fall within this category. And this situation brings us close to God and makes us His co-laborers.

Whether it be a desire to open a closed field, win a hostile tribe, obtain a better job, build a new church, have a successful meeting, rear a family, get through school or do any one of an almost infinite number of legitimate things, the method is likely to be the twofold one of work and prayer. We might paraphrase the famous exhortation of Dr. Simpson and say that when faced with these borderline tasks which we must work at but which we can never do alone, the thing to do is to work as if we had it all to do and pray as if we expected God to do it all.

But wishing—let the vain dreamers and the builders of Spanish castles spend their time at it if they will. We know better than to waste our time and efforts at anything so useless.

From *The Next Chapter after the Last*

(1987; repr., Camp Hill, PA: WingSpread, 2010)

EXPLORING WITH TOZER

Tozer rightly notes that wishing for a desired object or circumstance is not praying, since it does not usually bring itself to being submissive to God's will and God's timing. Wishing might be cute for children, but "the child should be taught very early that wishing gets him nowhere." Instead, if the desired object or circumstance is legitimate (i.e., not contrary to the Word of God), there are three possible ways for attaining it: work, prayer, or prayer and work (notice the switch in emphasis from work and prayer). However, before we delve into these three ways of getting what we want, we need to lay a solid foundation about prayer.

In Acts 6:4, the leadership of the early church recognized that they needed to "devote ourselves to prayer and to the ministry of the word." In Romans 12:12, believers are encouraged to rejoice in hope, persevere in tribulation, and to be "devoted to prayer." And again in Colossians 4:2, Paul writes under the leading of the Holy Spirit, "devote yourselves to prayer," which applies to all believers, not just leadership. This word "devoted" means to continue steadfastly in and give unremitting care to it, not just occasionally or for a season but continually in our walk of faith. The devotion to prayer in Colossians 4:2 is accompanied by the phrase, "keeping alert in it with an attitude of thanksgiving." This alertness or watchfulness is necessary since it is too easy to be distracted from praying at all. H. M. Carson noted the following about watchfulness and prayer:

Watchfulness suggests a danger to be avoided and this danger comes from two main quarters. The evil one makes the believer careless, so that he neglects the very practice of prayer, or on the other hand he dulls his mind or distracts his thoughts. Hence watchfulness means a disciplined attention to this continuous ministry, and it also involves a concentration of the whole being on its discharge.[1]

As such, the believer's devotion to prayer springs out of the constant fellowship with the Father and is as normal as breathing. The bottom line is that prayer undergirds everything for a believer: the situations where he must work, where the impossibility is so great that all he can do is pray and where he needs the wisdom of God to know how to pray, and where prayer and work need to be divinely balanced and timed such that God always gets the glory and honor for what He does.

May we remember that wishing leaves God out of the equation but praying puts Him into the equation and the solution if done according to His word and the leading of His Spirit.

REFLECT AND APPLY

1. "Some things are altogether out of the sphere of possibility for us, and yet altogether within God's gracious will for us. What to do? Prayer is the immediate answer. God has planned that we should go to Him for impossibilities when these impossibilities are part of His eternal will for our highest good." Reflect on those "impossibilities" where God answered your prayers. What was the commonality among the situations and the timing of

God's answers? How has or how should these past impossibilities encourage you to pray today?

2. On the other hand, "other things can be had by the simple expedient of work. It is useless to ask God for something we could obtain with a bit of effort properly directed. No instructed Christian will waste his time praying for things that are within his own power to obtain." With that being said, "whether, then, you eat or drink or whatever you do, do all to the glory of God" (1 Cor. 10:31). That means even in the simplest aspect of working for things that we want we must remain connected to the Father as we strive to please Him, to glorify Him, and to listen to Him for wisdom in every aspect of our simple work.

    I recall my own father, who maintained and repaired computers for many businesses. He had all of the training and enjoyed his work, but many times in the simple execution of his work he would come across problems and fixes that were beyond any computer manual. In those circumstances, he would pray and God would reveal a unique solution to the technical problem. God wants us ever connected to Him even in the simple expedient of daily work!

    Reflect on those times this week that you prayed in the midst of simple work. What was the extent of the prayer? What has been the frequency of such "arrow" prayers in your work? How does your answer to the previous question indicate the essence of your dependency upon Him?

3. The third category of getting desired objects adds up to work and prayer. "It will probably be

found that the greatest majority of desired objects and objectives fall within this category. And this situation brings us close to God and makes us His co-laborers." Personally, I see that prayer is first and then the work; but a continual repetition of this cycle is necessary for the work to move toward completion and for the believer to be moved even closer to the Lord. However, we need to be aware that the evil one wants us to be careless in our prayer life, dull of mind, and distracted. Can you remember a time when prayer and work was an ingrained part of your walk in Christ? Compare your current prayer and work to that time or better yet to what the Scriptures say in Colossians 4:2–6.

4. Meditate on the paraphrase of Dr. A. B. Simpson. "When faced with these borderline tasks which we must work at but which we can never do alone, the thing to do is to work as if we had it all to do and pray as if we expected God to do it all."

13

PRAYER CHANGES PEOPLE—AND THINGS

No one who has read the Bible with any perception can fail to see that to God, men and women are more important than things. A human being is of more value than a thousand galaxies of stars or a million worlds like ours. God made man in His own image and He made *things* to serve man. His concern is with intelligent moral beings, not with lifeless matter.

However, since every person has a material body and must live out his days in an environment of matter, time, and space, *things* are important to him. His earthly life is to a large degree interwoven with matter and the laws that control matter. He is often deeply affected by the report his senses bring him from the world around him. Situations sometimes develop where the welfare of the inner man is for the time allowed to depend somewhat upon outward circumstances. At such times it is altogether proper that he should pray to God to alter those circumstances and "change things" to afford a more favorable climate for the growth of the Spirit. A thousand promises are recorded in the Scriptures to encourage him to ask and seek and knock to the end so that unfavorable things might be changed or removed altogether. And the history of Israel and the church abundantly demonstrates that God does hear and answer prayer.

In all our praying, however, it is important that we keep in mind that God will not alter His eternal purposes at the word of a man. We do not pray in order to persuade God to change His mind. Prayer is not an assault upon the reluctance of God, nor an effort to secure a suspension of His will for us or for those for whom we pray. Prayer is not intended to overcome God and "move His arm." God will never be other than Himself, no matter how many people pray, nor how long nor how earnestly.

God's love desires the best for all of us, and He desires to give us the best at any cost. He will open rivers in desert places, still turbulent waves, quiet the wind, bring water from the rock, send an angel to release an apostle from prison, feed an orphanage, open a land long closed to the gospel. All these things and a thousand others He has done and will do in answer to prayer, but only because it had been His will to do it from the beginning. No one persuades Him.

What the praying man does is to bring His will into line with the will of God so God can do what He has all along been willing to do. Thus prayer changes the man and enables God to change things in answer to man's prayer.

From *The Price of Neglect*

(1991; repr., Camp Hill, PA: WingSpread, 2010)

EXPLORING WITH TOZER

God does not change, for Hebrews 13:8 says "Jesus Christ is the same yesterday and today and forever." He is just as sovereign, loving, omniscient, and merciful as He ever was. His Word, His promises, and His commands do not change. One of those commands was that "at all times they ought to pray" (Luke 18:1). Likewise, the apostle Paul commands under the power of the Holy Spirit to "pray without ceasing" (1 Thess. 5:17 and to "devote yourselves to prayer" (Col. 4:2). In the midst of God's unchangeable character and eternal purposes, we saints, who live in a world that is continually changing, are exhorted to pray. As we pray in the Spirit, we will begin to see people and things from the heavenly perspective. Of course, it will not happen immediately, but in the process of habitually praying in the Spirit, prayer will change us, the people in our sphere of influence, and things (for "He made things to serve man").

To illustrate these concepts, let us take a quick look at Abraham, who was called a friend of God in 2 Chronicles 20:7 and in James 2:23. The depths of this friendship with God are revealed in Genesis 18:17 when "the Lord said, 'Shall I hide from Abraham what I am about to do . . . ?'" Friends do not hide from each other! The Lord did not hide the truth that He was going to destroy Sodom and Gomorrah, but Abraham lingered before the Lord and prayed. It was a petition nestled in the constraints of God's character, but seasoned with persistence, boldness, humility, and a sense of closure to the request. This whole prayer experience changed Abraham, Lot, Lot's family, and all the people in Abraham's sphere of influence. But even more, it changed not only Abraham's walk with the Lord but his prayer life (see Gen. 20:7, 17). May we be willing to embrace such change to further God's glory!

REFLECT AND APPLY

1. "A human being is of more value than a thousand galaxies of stars or a million worlds like ours. God made man in His own image and He made things to serve man. His concern is with intelligent moral beings, not with lifeless matter." Reflect on this statement. What value does it add, now and later, to our prayers for people and things?

2. "We do not pray in order to persuade God to change His mind. Prayer is not an assault upon the reluctance of God, nor an effort to secure a suspension of His will for us or for those for whom we pray. Prayer is not intended to overcome God and 'move His arm.' God will never be other than Himself, no matter how many people pray, nor how long nor how earnestly." In light of this comment, how do you explain Abraham's prayer for Lot and Sodom and Gomorrah? Consider one thing that you have persistently been praying about. Have you been trying to coerce God or is your request nestled in His will? What is the value of asking ourselves such questions?

3. "All these things and a thousand others He has done and will do in answer to prayer, but only because it had been His will to do it from the beginning. No one persuades Him." Reflect on three answered prayers in the past six months or weeks

as to what your prayer was, what God answered, and what promises you stood on. What commonalities did these prayers have?

4. "What the praying man does is to bring His will into line with the will of God so God can do what He has all along been willing to do. Thus prayer changes the man and enables God to change things in answers to man's prayer." Where does the Word of God come into this equation? It is possible that feeble praying these days is related to being babes in the Word. Meditate on Hebrews 5:11–14.

14

ON WRESTLING
IN PRAYER

There is an idea abroad that wrestling in prayer is always a good thing, but that is by no means true. Extreme religious exercises may be undergone with no higher motive than to get our own way.

The spiritual quality of a prayer is determined not by its intensity but by its origin. In evaluating prayer we should inquire who is doing the praying—our determined hearts or the Holy Spirit. If the prayer originates with the Holy Spirit, then the wrestling can be beautiful and wonderful; but if we are the victims of our own overheated desires, our praying can be as carnal as any other act.

Two examples are given in the Old Testament, Jacob and the prophets of Baal. Jacob's wrestling was a real exercise, and at first it was not Jacob's doing. "And Jacob was left alone; and there wrestled a man with him until the breaking of the day." Obviously the "man" was the aggressor, not Jacob, but when Jacob had been beaten upon, he became the aggressor and cried, "I will not let thee go, except thou bless me" (32:24, 26). The wrestling was of divine origin, and the blessed results are known to every Bible student.

The other example does not turn out so well. The prophets of Baal wrestled also, much more violently than Jacob, but they wrestled in the flesh. Their writhings were born of ignorance and superstition and got them nowhere. Everything was a mistake—their zeal, their body-punishing prayer, their determination. They were wrong in spite of their zealous praying. And such error did not die with them.

Only the Spirit can pray effectively. "Likewise the Spirit also helpeth our infirmities: for we know not what we should pray for as we ought: but the Spirit itself maketh intercession for us with groanings which cannot be uttered" (Rom. 8:26).

From *The World: Playground or Battleground*
(1989; repr., Camp Hill, PA: WingSpread, 2009)

EXPLORING WITH TOZER

Hosea 12: 3–4 gives us a quick snapshot of Jacob's life of wrestling: "In the womb he took his brother by the heel, and in his maturity he contended with God. Yes, he wrestled with the angel and prevailed."

Jacob's entire life had been one of wrestling for God's blessings through deceitful or fleshly means, as illustrated by his deceitful gain of Esau's birthright and the stealing of his father's blessing. And yet at the ford of the Jabbok River, Jacob is cornered in his fears and past sins with no way out; so he prays and sends his brother a gift (Gen. 32:9–23). He prays by reminding God of His promises in humility, as he quickly recalls God's mercies and faithfulness to him over all of the years even in spite of his scheming; and in earnest as he asks for God's deliverance. This prayer is followed by his last attempts to placate his brother's anger at his past deceitful schemes, which is typical of us all when we continually dip into the schemes and plans which have worked in the past but that leave God out.

While alone that evening with all of his fears, Jacob and the man or the angel (the angel of the Lord) wrestled until daylight. Jacob would not let the angel go even after Jacob's thigh was dislocated. In fact, he would not let go until blessed. The words of the angel were that "Your name shall no longer be Jacob [the supplanter], but Israel; for you have striven with God and with men and have prevailed" (v. 28). Significantly, *Israel* means "one who strives with God," or "God strives." This striving with God did not originate in Jacob's determined heart but with God Himself, as He was the initiator in this wrestling.

We all tend to wrestle with God in prayer with determined hearts, trying to obtain the answer to our prayer our way and in our timing. We mouth the words and thoughts that we want God's will in our prayer, but the reality is that we want to get our own way, which is never the divinely optimum. However, if we are anxious to pursue God's will for our lives, He will allow us each to be hemmed in by some situation where there is no escape or solution apart from Him. It is in this tight place that the prayer originates with the Holy Spirit as we submit to God (James 4:7–8). The end result is a wrestling with God that is beautiful and wonderful in that God is glorified, God's best option is executed for all involved, our prayer life is enriched, and our dependence upon Him takes a step forward.

Similar thoughts are expressed in Colossians 4:12–13 where Epaphras is "always laboring earnestly for you in his prayers, that you may stand perfect and fully assured in all the will of God. For I testify for him that he has a deep concern for you." This Greek word for "laboring earnestly" was used to describe athletes as they gave themselves fully to their sport, thus capturing the essence of wrestling in prayer for others. The conviction that comes from Paul's words under the inspiration of the Holy Spirit is that there are few that pray this way, and thus this is another strong reason for why revival tarries.

REFLECT AND APPLY

1. One must be ever vigilant to avoid "extreme religious exercises [that] may be undergone with no higher motive than to get our own way." Can you remember a situation that prompted you to pray more frequently and fervently in the past two to six months? Did you feel hemmed in? Did you notice a change in your petition or prayers as you waited for God's answer? (If so, what was the change?) And lastly, why is this sense of being hemmed in by fears or circumstances so critical to us in wrestling in prayer?

2. The following questions are intended to encourage us to step back and ask God to search our

hearts as to the origin of our prayers. First, is the origin of our prayer our determined heart or is it a burden that God the Holy Spirit has laid on us? As Tozer writes, "If the prayer originates with the Holy Spirit, then the wrestling can be beautiful and wonderful." The end result is that we eventually get not only what God laid on our heart, but we also get to know God better, we progress in our prayer life, and we begin to see more as God sees. Second, if the origin of our prayer is "our own overheated desires," then do we not need to expose that prayer for what it is: unholy, carnal, and blasphemous? Exposure of this kind of praying can bring freedom to the believer in his relationship to the Father and enable him to see God do even greater things. Non-exposure of this kind of praying has opposite effects. We all need a mentor to help us see such blind spots in our lives and prayer. Pray for God to provide one!

3. Not only must the origin of the wrestling in prayer be divine, but the wrestling itself must be done in the power of the Holy Spirit. Reflect on some important prayers that God may have placed on your heart over the past six months. As you prayed persistently, did you come away with a sense of exhaustion? Was the exhaustion because of worry or concern that things were not going to turn out as you prayed? Reflect on Psalm 55:22: "Cast your burden upon the Lord and He will sustain you; He will never allow the righteous to be shaken [or tottered]." If you have not done this, do so right now.

4. Paul writes in Colossians 4:12–13 that "Epaphras, who is one of your number, a bondslave of Jesus

Christ, sends you his greetings, always laboring earnestly for you in his prayers, that you may stand perfect and fully assured in all the will of God. For I testify for him that he has a deep concern for you." Meditate on the origin, the wrestling, the motivation, and the content of his prayer and make it yours!

15

PRAYING TILL
WE PRAY

D r. Moody Stuart, a great praying man of a past generation, once drew up a set of rules to guide him in his prayers. Among these rules is this one: "Pray till you pray."

The difference between praying till you quit and praying till you pray is illustrated by the American evangelist John Wesley Lee. He often likened a season of prayer to a church service, and insisted that many of us close the meeting before the service is over. He confessed that once he arose too soon from a prayer session and started down the street to take care of some pressing business. He had only gone a short distance when an inner voice reproached him. "Son," the voice seemed to say, "did you not pronounce the benediction before the meeting was ended?" He understood, and at once hurried back to the place of prayer where he tarried till the burden lifted and the blessing came down.

The habit of breaking off our prayers before we have truly prayed is as common as it is unfortunate. Often the last ten minutes may mean more to us than the first half hour, because we must spend a long time getting into the proper mood to pray effectively. We may need to struggle with our thoughts to draw them in from where they have been scattered through the multitude of distractions that result from the task of living in a disordered world.

Here, as elsewhere in spiritual matters, we must be sure to distinguish the ideal from the real. Ideally we should be living moment-by-moment in a state of such perfect union with God that no special preparation is necessary. But actually there are few who can honestly say that this is their experience. Candor will compel most of us to admit that we often experience a struggle before we can escape from the emotional alienation and sense of unreality that sometimes settle over us as a sort of prevailing mood.

Whatever a dreamy idealism may say, we are forced to deal with things down on the level of practical reality. If when we come to prayer our hearts feel dull and unspiritual, we should not try to argue ourselves out of it. Rather, we should admit it frankly and pray our way through. Some Christians smile at the thought of "praying through," but something of the same idea is found in the writings of practically every great praying saint from Daniel to the present day. We cannot afford to stop praying till we have actually prayed.

The World: Playground or Battleground?
(1989; repr., Camp Hill, PA: WingSpread, 2009)

EXPLORING WITH TOZER

The sense of Tozer's meaning in this pensive writing is that true, effective prayer is cloaked in honesty, and the one who prays struggles through distractions and hurdles and is not confined by tight time constraints, proceeding past the formality of five minutes of running through our prayer list. Instead one takes the time to listen and respond to God's voice. This results in the burden(s) being laid at the foot of the cross and in a peace of heart that floods the soul of the one who knows he has been heard.

D. A. Carson notes that to "pray until you pray" was Puritan advice and makes the following interpretation of it in practice:

Christians should pray long enough and honestly enough, at a single session, to get past the feelings of formalism and unreality that attends not a little praying. We are especially prone to such feelings when we pray for only a few minutes, rushing to be done with a mere duty. To enter the spirit of prayer, we must stick to it for a while. If we "pray until we pray," eventually we come to delight in God's presence, to rest in His love, to cherish His will. Even in dark or agonized praying, we somehow know we are doing business with God. In short, we discover a little of what Jude means when he exhorts his readers to "pray in the Holy Spirit" (Jude 20)—which presumably means it is treacherously possible to pray not in the Spirit.[1]

The end result of *not* praying until you pray is that we throw requests at God not grounded in the Scriptures, potentially not in His will, and with hope some of the requests will stick and be answered. We end up missing our awesome God and fellowship with Him.

In the Scriptures we find many examples of men who prayed until they prayed, but we will mention only three: Elijah, Nehemiah, and Daniel. We know from James 5:16–18 that Elijah was such a man of prayer.

The effective prayer of a righteous man can accomplish much. Elijah was a man with a nature like ours, and he prayed earnestly that it would not rain, and it did not rain on the earth for three years and six months. Then he prayed again and the sky poured rain and the earth produced its fruit.

Elijah lived with the tension of his prayer for no rain for three and a half years, and then one day he knew the time had come in the contest with the prophets of Baal (1 Kings 18). The prophets of Baal prayed, leaped before their altar, and mutilated themselves; but there was no answer. Elijah prayed with humility standing on the character of God, which is unchanging and ever faithful to His Word. His final petition was that "this people may know that You, O Lord, are God, and that You have turned their heart back again," and God answered in a mighty way.

Similarly Nehemiah prayed for Jerusalem and the Jews there for about four months before God gave opportunity to provide an answer.

The book of Daniel is filled with prayer, but Daniel 9 specifically addresses his prayer for Israel and her people as he prayed until he prayed. His prayer contained praise of our perfect God, confession, focus on the character of God versus our unfaithfulness and disobedience, understanding of God's discipline for our waywardness over time, and finally petitions.

May we learn to "pray until we pray" as these prophets of old did. Steps in this direction will expand our faith in a great God!

REFLECT AND APPLY

1. "The habit of breaking off our prayers before we have truly prayed is as common as it is unfortunate." Take the past week of your prayer life and assess it in this regard. Was the breaking off of your prayers due to time issues? Was it due to distractions or seemingly urgent things that needed to be dealt with? Was it due to not budgeting time or having disciplined choices or maybe combinations of them all? Whatever the reason or reasons for not being able to "pray until you pray," ask God to enable you to make changes in your prayer time so that you can experience Him as you "pray until you pray."

2. "If when we come to prayer our hearts feel dull and unscriptural, we should not try to argue ourselves out of it. Rather, we should admit it frankly and pray our way through." We have all found ourselves in this position at some time, perhaps even frequently. Notice that Tozer is suggesting honesty before the throne of grace and a refocus on the One who "always lives to make intercession

for [us]" (Heb. 7:25). Write down your prayers for a week or a few days and allow God's Spirit some time to allow you to see your honesty before God and your heart to pray through.

3. Just possibly our five-minute prayer time is not being done in the power of the Holy Spirit. As a result, there is no way we can "pray until you pray." How does one assess this major deviation from "pray at all times in the Spirit?" (Eph. 6:18). First, this assessment cannot be done fully by us. We need a mentor who will not only look at our prayer life but our walk with the Lord in total. Second, this evaluation process will take humility, repentance, and time as the Lord renews our minds, hearts, and our prayer life. For sure, we will know Him better at the end of it and will be more concerned with what His concerns are. Take some steps in finding that mentor and beginning that evaluation process.

16

GOD'S SELFHOOD AND PRAYER

Did you ever think about God without getting down on your knees and begging for something? Most of us, when we pray, bring our grocery list and say, "Lord, we'd like this and this and this." We act as if we were running to the corner store to get something. And God has been dragged down in our thinking to nothing more than the One who gives us what we want when we're in trouble.

Now God does give us what we want—He's a good God. God's goodness is one of His attributes. But I hope that we'll not imagine that God exists simply to answer the prayers of people. A businessman wants to get a contract, so he goes to God and says, "God, give me." A student wants to get a good grade, so she goes to God and says, "Give me." A young man wants the girl to say yes, so he gets on his knees and says, "Father, give her to me." We just *use* God as a kind of source of getting what we want.

Our heavenly Father is very kind and He tells us that we are to ask. Whatever we ask in the name of His Son He'll give us, if it's within the confines of His will. And His will is as broad as the whole world. Still, we must think of God as the Holy One, not just as the One from whom we can get things. God is not a glorified Santa Claus, who gives us everything we want, then fades out and lets us run our own way. He gives, but in giving He gives us Himself too. And the best gift God ever gives us is Himself. He gives answers to prayer, but after we've used up the answer or don't need it anymore, we still have God.

In God's self there is no sin. We creatures properly and rightly and scripturally have everything to say against self and selfishness—it's the great sin. But God's self is not sinful, because God is the original, unfallen, holy God. The poet says,

> In Thy praise of Self untiring
> Thy perfections shine;
> Self-sufficient, self-admiring,—
> Such life must be Thine—
> Glorifying Self, yet blameless
> With a sanctity all shameless
> It is so divine![1]

God loves Himself—the Father loves the Son, the Son loves the Father, and the Son and the Father love the Holy Spirit. They understood this in the olden times, when men were thinkers instead of imitators and they thought within the confines of the Bible.

Incidentally, in discussing God's attributes I am not trying to think my way up to God. You can't think your way up to God any more than you can climb a ladder to the moon. You can't think your way into the kingdom of heaven—you go in by faith. But after you're in you can think about the kingdom of heaven. You can't think your way to England, but after you get there you can think about England.

So God loves Himself. And He loves Himself because He is the God who originated love. He is the I AM of love, the essence of all holiness, and the fountain of all self-conscious light.

The words "I" and "I am" always refer to the self. I knew a dear old brother—God bless him, he's in heaven now and he'll wear a crown so big that it'll come down over my shoulders, I'm sure—he'd been a missionary to China and he didn't believe much in saying "I." He knew that "I" meant self, and a fallen self is a sinful thing, so he would always say "one." And he'd say things like, "When one was in China one said this, and one did this." He meant himself—he was afraid to say "I." I suppose if he'd been writing Psalm 23, he'd make it read like this: "The Lord is one's Shepherd, one shall not want."

There's nothing wrong with saying "I" or "I am." But when you say, "I am," you always put "am" in lowercase letters. But when God said, "I AM," He put it in capitals—there's a difference. When God says, "I AM," it means He did not derive from anywhere. He started the whole business—He is God. But when I say "I am," I'm a little echo of God.

I believe that God is very proud of His children. I believe that throughout the vast reaches of this universe God is happy to call His people His people. Do you remember what God said about Job? The sons of God—the angels—were all passing in parade, and who comes with them but Satan himself. The brass, the arrogance that he had—traveling along with the unfallen sons of God! And when he got out before the reviewing stand, God said, "Have you seen my servant Job? He is a good man and eschews evil. Have you seen my servant Job?" [see Job 1:8]. He was proud of Job.

God is proud of His people, and He's proud to have us say, "I am" in a little echo voice, because He is the original Voice who said "I AM THAT I AM." The doctrine that man has been made in the image of God is one of the basic doctrines of the Bible and one of the most elevating, enlarging, magnanimous and glorious doctrines that I know. There's nothing wrong with self-respect, there's nothing wrong with saying, "I am" and "I will" and "I do" as long as we remember we're saying it in lowercase letters, as an echo from the original One who first said, "I AM."

Strange, isn't it, that God the Son was called the Word and God enabled man to speak. And he enabled no other creature to speak. Not the finest-bred dog can talk, not the finest myna bird (they're supposed to talk, but they don't know what they're saying). Man alone can talk, because only man has this thing we call the *logos*—the Word.

The essence of sin is independent self. You see, God sat on the throne—the I AM. And along came man and said, "I will" and sought to rise above the throne of God. He disobeyed God and took the bit in his own teeth and became a little god in his own right. The sinful world says, "I am," forgetting that they are an echo of the One above and saying it in their own right.

The definition of sin is fallen selfhood. God is the great "Sun of righteousness" (Mal. 4:2), And around Him, warmed and healed by His holy Person, all His creatures move—all the seraphim, cherubim, angels, archangels, children of God and watchers in the skies. And best of all is man, made in His own image.

Once we revolved around God as a planet around its sun. Then one day the little planet said, "I'll be my own sun. Away with this God." And man fell. That's what we call the fall of man. Sin reached up and took God's self and said, "I'll be self myself." And God was ruled out. As the holy apostle said, they did not like to have God in their minds, therefore God gave them over to vile affections (Rom. 1:26). All the evil that the police, educators, doctors, and psychiatrists are worried about now—deviancy, sodomy, exhibitionism and all the rest—all came as a result of man not wanting to have this God in his mind or in his heart, not recognizing Him as being God. He went out on his own to be his own little god.

Isn't that the way the average sinner acts? He's his own little god. He's the sun. He puts himself in capital letters and forgets that there's anybody up there that'll judge him.

Sin has symptoms and manifestations, just as cancer has certain manifestations. Paul gives a list of them in Galatians 5:19–21: "Now the works of the flesh are manifest, which are these; Adultery, fornication, uncleanness, lasciviousness, idolatry, witchcraft, hatred, variance, emulations, wrath, strife, seditions, heresies, envyings, murders, drunkenness, revellings, and such like."

These things are all symptoms of something deeper: our asserting self. It is asserting my created and derived self, putting myself on the throne and saying, "I am self: I am that I am."

I have read books on existentialism. I could shudder and grieve that men can be so tragically mistaken as they are, and yet I knew they were because I read my Bible. Existentialists say that man is—man wasn't created, man just *is*—and he has to start from there. He has no Creator, no planner, nobody that thought him out: he just *is*. They make man say what only God can say: "I am that I am." Man can say, in a modest humble voice, "I am," but only God can say in capital letters, "I AM THAT I AM." Man has forgotten that and that is sin.

It is not your temper that is sin; it's something deeper than your temper. It is not your lust that is sin; it's something deeper than that—that's but a symptom. All the crime in the world—all the evil, the robberies, the rapes, the desertions, the assassinations—they're but the external manifestations of an inward disease: sin.

And yet, it is not to be thought of as a disease so much as an attitude, a derangement. There sat God upon His throne, the I AM THAT I AM, the eternal self-sufficient, self-existent One. He made man to be like Him and gave him a will—He said, "Man can do as he pleases." He meant for man to circle around the throne of God as the planets circle around the sun. But man said, "I am that I am"—he turned away from God, and fallen self took over. No matter how many manifestations sin may have, remember that the liquid essence in the bottle is always self.

That's why it's not always easy to get people to become real Christians. You can get them to sign a card, or make a decision, or join a church, or something like that. But to get people delivered from their sin is a pretty hard deal because it means that I've got to get off that throne. God belongs on that throne but sin has pushed God off and taken over.

Can you imagine it? The great God Almighty, maker of heaven and earth, said, "This is My name throughout all generations, My memorial forever: I AM THAT I AM. I never was created; I was not made, I AM. I made you for My love. I made you to worship, honor and glorify Me. I made you to love you and hold you and give Myself to you. But you turned away from Me. And you made yourself god and you put yourself on that throne." That is sin.

That's why the Scripture says, "Except a man be born again, he cannot see the kingdom of God" (John 3:3). What does "born again" mean? Among other things, it means a renewal, a rebirth, but it also means getting off the throne and putting God on it. It means that the self-existent One is recognized for who He is.

Long ago there was one by the name of Lucifer, to whom God gave a position higher than any other creature—at the very throne of God. One day pride took over and he said, "I will arise, I will set my throne above God's throne." And he became proud and God cast him down (see Isa. 14:12–14). That's the devil.

And it is the devil who is leading the world now, "the prince of the power of the air, the spirit that now worketh in the children of disobedience" (Eph. 2:2), right out there among the leaders of society, our politicians, our literary men and all the rest. This is true not only in North America, but all over the world from the day Adam sinned. We're guilty of offending His majesty, of insulting the Royalty that sits upon the eternal, uncreated throne. We're guilty of sacrilegious rebellion.

You've been saying, "I AM THAT I AM," in capital letters, when you should say meekly and reverently, "O God, I am because Thou art." That's what the new birth means. It means repentance and faith.

From *The Attributes of God*, vol. 2
(2003; repr., Chicago: Moody, 2015)

EXPLORING WITH TOZER

E very good thing given and every perfect gift is from above, coming from the Father of lights, with whom there is no variation or shifting shadow" (James 1:17). This verse firmly establishes God as the giver of only good things (even if we cannot see the good in the gift initially), of perfect gifts from Him, and of gifts that keep on coming (i.e., God does not just give occasionally but constantly). Foundational to these truths is the unchangeableness of God. God does not change! He is "the same yesterday and today and forever" (Heb. 13:8). Thus our focus in prayer should not be so much on our prayer list or a get list, but on the God behind all of the giving.

Let us ever remember the story of the ten lepers who cried unto Jesus for mercy and the one leper who honored God:

When He saw them, He said to them, "Go and show yourselves to the priests." And as they were going, they were cleansed. Now one of them, when he saw that he had been healed, turned back, glorifying God with a loud voice, and he fell on his face at His feet, giving thanks to Him. And he was a Samaritan. Then Jesus answered and said, "Were there not ten cleansed? But the nine—where are they? Was no one found who returned to give glory to God, except this foreigner?" And He said to him, "Stand up and go; your faith has made you well." (Luke 17:14–19)

This Samaritan leper had a grocery list of one item, but he got much more as he came back to the Savior with humility, worship, and thankfulness. He sought a gift from the Savior but got to know the Giver of all behind the gift as well as knowing that his faith was increased. In contrast, our short prayer times and our prayer lists, which seem to be just grocery lists, can undermine us in really getting to know our God behind the gift that we sought. In addition, our faith does not grow and our prayers become ever more stagnant and self-focused. May we strive in the power of the Holy Spirit to know God's great goodness toward us as reflected in His good, perfect, and consistent gifts to us.

REFLECT AND APPLY

1. Do an honest assessment of your prayer times in asking of God. Is it like a grocery list or a "get" list? Of course, most grocery lists are put together in hopes of getting everything on the list. Among those grocery lists are priorities, wish items, and not-so-important items. Do you have a freedom to focus on just one item on that list—or on another item not even on the list that God the Holy Spirit has impressed your spirit to pray about? There is nothing wrong with a listing to aid this weak flesh to recall, but one must be careful that a list doesn't become a legalistic tool to get our prayer time with God done quickly. Has your list driven you to react as the Samaritan leper did? If not, consider ways to restructure your prayer times with God.

2. "Now God does give us what we want—He's a good God. God's goodness is one of His attributes." His goodness and unchangeableness are two rich truths about His character that should enrich our times in prayer. Do you come away from your prayer list presentation to God satisfied that you remembered the list and got through it? Or do you come away with a confidence that you have been heard, with a sense that some of your requests have been edited and restructured before God as you have talked with Him, and with a deep peace which surpasses all comprehension? (Phil. 4:6–7). Has your perspective of God been expanded and your faith renewed or increased? These kinds of questions cannot be answered in evaluating one prayer time, but over a month or two of such evaluations we may see things more clearly. Ask God to change your prayer times; but if still struggling after a few months, seek assistance from a more mature believer.

3. "God is not a glorified Santa Claus, who gives us everything we want, then fades outs and lets us run our way. He gives, but in giving He gives of Himself too. And the best gift God ever gives us is Himself. He gives answers to prayer, but after we've used up the answer or don't need it anymore, we still have God." Reflect on whether you have been realizing that gift of God Himself in your prayer life. Or have you been so self-centered on the gift that you have missed the Giver of the gift? If it is the latter, ask God for forgiveness and for change in your heart and prayer time.

TRUTH HAS
TWO WINGS

Truth is like a bird; it cannot fly with one wing. Yet we are forever trying to take off with one wing flapping furiously and the other tucked neatly out of sight.

I believe it was Dr. G. Campbell Morgan who said that "the whole truth does not lie in 'It is written,' but in 'It is written,' and 'Again it is written.'" The second text must be placed over against the first to balance it and give it symmetry, just as the right wing must work along with the left to balance the bird and enable it to fly.

Many of the doctrinal divisions among the churches are the result of a blind and stubborn insistence that truth has but one wing. Each side holds tenaciously to one text, refusing grimly to acknowledge the validity of the other. This error is an evil among churches, but it is a real tragedy when it gets into the hearts of individual Christians and begins to affect their devotional lives.

Lack of balance in the Christian life is often the direct

consequence of overemphasis on certain favorite texts, with a corresponding underemphasis on other related ones. For it is not denial only that makes a truth void; failure to emphasize it will in the long run be equally damaging. And this puts us in the odd position of holding a truth theoretically while we make it of no effect by neglecting it in practice. Unused truth becomes as useless as an unused muscle.

Sometimes our dogmatic insistence upon "It is written" and our refusal to hear "Again it is written" makes heretics of us, our heresy being the noncreedal variety which does not rouse the opposition of the theologians. One example of this is the teaching that crops up now and again having to do with confession of sin. It goes like this: Christ died for our sins, not only for all we have committed but for all we may yet commit for the remainder of our lives. When we accept Christ we receive the benefit of everything He did for us in His dying and rising again. In Christ all our current sins are forgiven beforehand. It is therefore unnecessary for us to confess our sins. In Christ they are already forgiven.

Now, this is completely wrong, and it is all the more wrong because it is half right. It is true that Christ died for all our sins, but it is not true that because Christ died for *all* our sins we need not confess that we have sinned when we have. This conclusion does not follow from that premise.

It is written that Christ died for our sins, and again it is written that "if we confess our sins, he is faithful and just to forgive us our sins" (1 John 1:9). These two texts are written of the same company of persons, namely Christians. We dare not compel the first text to invalidate the second. Both are true and one completes the other. The meaning of the two is that since Christ died for our sins, if we confess our sins they will be forgiven. To teach otherwise is to attempt to fly with one wing.

Another example: I have met some who claim that it is wrong to pray for the same thing twice, the reason being that if we truly believe when we pray we have the answer the first time; any second prayer betrays the unbelief of the first; therefore, let there be no second prayer.

Three things are wrong with this teaching. First, it ignores a large body of Scripture; second, it rarely works in practice, even for the saintliest soul; and, third, if persisted in, it robs the praying man of two of his mightiest weapons in his warfare of the flesh and the devil, specifically, intercession and petition.

For let it be said without qualification that the effective intercessor is never a one-prayer man, neither does the successful petitioner win his mighty victory in his first attempt. Had David subscribed to the one-prayer creed he could have reduced his psalms to about one-third their present length. Elijah would not have prayed seven times for rain (and incidentally, there would have been no rain, either). Our Lord would not have prayed the third time, saying the same words, nor would Paul have "besought the Lord thrice" (2 Cor. 12:8) for the removal of his "thorn." In fact, if this teaching were true, much wonderful biblical narrative would have to be rewritten, for the Bible has much to say about continued and persistent prayer.

One thing hidden in such teachings is unconscious spiritual pride. The Christian who refuses to confess sin on the ground that it is already forgiven is setting himself above prophets and psalmists and all the saints who have left anything on record about themselves from Paul to the present time. These did not hide their sins behind a syllogism, but eagerly and fully confessed them. Perhaps that is why they were such great souls and those who claim to have found a better way are so small.

And one has but to note the smug smile of superiority on the face of the one-prayer Christian to sense that there is a lot of pride behind the smile. While other Christians wrestle with God in an agony of intercession, one-prayer Christians sit back in humble pride waiting it out. They do not pray because they have already prayed. The devil has no fear of such Christians. He has already won over them, and his technique has been false logic.

Let's use both wings. We'll get farther that way.

From *That Incredible Christian*
(1964; repr., Camp Hill, PA: WingSpread, 2008).

EXPLORING WITH TOZER

This chapter on truth seems to be initially out of place on prayer but is very appropriate since we tend to have some misconceptions about prayer that are rooted in not knowing the whole truth as revealed in Scripture and as noted by Tozer, who quotes Campbell Morgan: "The whole truth does not lie in 'It is written,' but in 'It is written' and 'Again, it is written.' The second text must be placed against the first to balance it and give it symmetry, just as the right wing must work along with the left to balance the bird and enable it to fly."

This lack of balance, or symmetry, in truth can distort our prayer life in very subtle ways. For instance, our pride might be elevated, our faith weakened, our zeal for God's best damaged, our perspectives of God and His ways undermined, and our day-by-day communion with God compromised.

Maybe one way to assess these imbalances is to evaluate these truths with several tests. First, who gets the glory? Is it God or man? Is my smugness increased as a result of just praying once? Second, is my communion with God enriched with the imbalance in my prayer? Is my prayer time often one-sided, with no sense of hearing God speak? Third, is there a supernatural element to the answers to my prayers, or do I take credit for God putting me in the right spot at the right time? Of course, this latter component can be true from time to time, but there is a supernatural component to that placement. Fourth, do I feel a greater burden to pray more about friends, family, strangers, and passing situations? Or do I feel content to just pray about people and things in my immediate sphere of influence?

Finally, do I have the eyes of faith to see the spiritual battle around me? Am I experiencing the attacks of the evil one or is he leaving me alone since he has rendered me ineffective before the throne of grace?

A very powerful passage of Scripture that focuses on this balance and symmetry in prayer is James 4:1–10. Notice especially James's admonition in verses 6–10: "'God is opposed to the proud, but gives grace to the humble.' Submit therefore to God. Resist the devil and he will flee from you. Draw near to God and He will draw near to you. . . . Humble yourselves in the presence of the Lord, and He will exalt you."

If we are spiraling away either slowly or quickly from our Father in heaven, may we snuggle close to Him and He will draw near to us. That is His promise!

REFLECT AND APPLY

1. The only misconception that Tozer deals with on prayer here is "the claim that it is wrong to pray for the same thing twice," for if we say we believe in the first prayer, the second prayer betrays the unbelief of the first. Reflect on Tozer's answers from Scriptures. How would you respond to a believer who had this misconception?

2. Another misconception that some believers hide behind (though not addressed by Tozer) is the sovereignty of God. For instance, since God is sovereign, why should we pray? What is the balanced or symmetrical perspective of the sovereignty of God in prayer? How has this two-winged truth on the sovereignty of God enriched or emboldened your prayers? In addition, ask God to expose any other misconceptions in your prayer life.

3 James 4:1–10 is a rich passage on prayer that would be worthwhile to commit to memory. For instance, do you ask yourself why you do request of God certain things? Is it because you are afraid of the answer or because you think you know the answer or because you are unconsciously or consciously going to do it your way? On the other side, do you evaluate why you did not receive what you asked for? The whole intent of these questions is not to make us introspective so we

cannot pray with the freedom of the Spirit but to allow the Spirit of God to search our hearts to expose motives and perspectives that are not honoring to God.

4. "Humble yourselves in the presence of the Lord, and He will exalt you" (James 4:10). For the next week, meditate and pray over this verse and its meaning for you.

18

HONESTY
IN PRAYER

The saintly David M'Intyre, in his radiant little book, *The Hidden Life of Prayer,* deals frankly, if briefly, with a vital element of true prayer which in our artificial age is likely to be overlooked. We mean just plain honesty. "Honest dealing becomes us," says M'Intyre, "when we kneel in His pure presence." He continues,

> In our address to God, we like to speak of Him as we think we ought to speak, and there are times when our words far outrun our feelings. But it is best that we should be perfectly frank before Him. He will allow us to say anything we will, so long as it is to Himself. "I will say unto God my rock," exclaims the psalmist, "why hast thou forgotten me?" If he had said, "Lord, thou canst not forget. Thou hast graven my name on the palms of thy hands," he would have spoken more worthily, but less truly.

On one occasion Jeremiah failed to interpret God aright. He cried as if in anger, "O Lord, you deceived me, and I was deceived." These are terrible words to utter before Him who is changeless truth. But the prophet spoke as he felt, and the Lord not only pardoned him, but met him and blessed him there.[1]

Another spiritual writer of unusual penetration has advised frankness in prayer even to a degree that might appear to be downright rudeness. When you come to prayer, he says, and find that you have no taste for it, tell God so without mincing words. If God and spiritual things bore you, admit it frankly. This advice will shock some squeamish saints, but it is altogether sound nevertheless. God loves the guileless soul even when in his ignorance he is actually guilty of rashness in prayer. The Lord can soon cure his ignorance, but for insincerity no cure is known.

The basic artificiality of civilized human beings is hard to shake off. It gets into our very blood and conditions our thoughts, attitudes, and relationships much more seriously than we imagine. A book on human relations has appeared within recent years whose underlying philosophy is deception and whose recommended technique is a skillful use of flattery to gain desired ends. It has had an unbelievably wide sale, actually running into the millions. Of course its popularity may be explained by the fact that it said what people wanted to hear.

The desire to make a good impression has become one of the most powerful of all the factors determining human conduct. That gracious (and scriptural) social lubricant called courtesy has in our times degenerated into a completely false and phony etiquette that hides the true man under a shimmery surface as thin as the oil slick on a quiet pond. The only time some persons expose their real self is when they get mad.

With this perverted courtesy determining almost everything men say and do in human society, it is not surprising that it should be hard to be completely honest in our relations with God. It carries over as a kind of mental reflex and is present without our being aware of it. Nevertheless, it is extremely hateful to God. Christ detested it and condemned it without mercy when He found it among the Pharisees. The artless little child is still the divine model for all of us. Prayer will increase in power and reality as we repudiate all pretense and learn to be utterly honest before God as well as before men.

A great Christian of the past broke out all at once into a place of such radiance and victory as to excite wonder among his friends. Someone asked him what had happened to him. He replied simply that his new life of power began one day when he entered the presence of God and took a solemn vow never again to say anything to God in prayer that he did not mean. His transformation began with that vow and continued as he kept it.

We can learn something there if we will.

From *God Tells the Man Who Cares*
(1993; repr., Camp Hill, PA: WingSpread, 2010)

EXPLORING WITH TOZER

In our age of artificiality, fantasies, and concerns with appearances, just plain honesty is hard to find. As true believers in Christ, we should not misrepresent truth in order to mislead others or even ourselves. Honesty and deceit cannot coexist! We know from Isaiah 53:9 that there was never any deceit in our Savior's mouth. Recall also that Jesus commended Nathanael by saying,: "Behold, an Israelite indeed, in whom there is no deceit!" (John 1:47). Maybe we should all ask ourselves if Jesus Christ would commend us for the lack of deceit in our walk and our prayer life.

Likewise, we are told in Romans 1:28–29 that those who do not acknowledge God any longer are continually "filled with all unrighteousness, wickedness, greed, evil . . . envy, murder, strife, deceit, malice." As true believers, we are "sons of light and sons of day. We are not of night nor of darkness" (1 Thess. 5:5). Thus, we should not adopt or have any part in the deceitful ways of the world, which will affect our prayer life. In that light, Tozer makes the strong case that honesty before God in prayer transforms the believer's walk in Christ and his prayer life. François Fénelon, a seventeenth-century French priest, made some powerful statements about this honesty before God in prayer:

> Tell God all that is in your heart, as one unloads one's heart, its pleasures and its pains, to a dear friend. Tell Him your troubles that He may comfort you; tell Him your longings that He may purify them; tell Him your dislikes that He may help you conquer them; tell Him your temptations

that He may shield you from them; show Him the wounds of your soul that He may heal them; lay bare your indifference to good, your depraved taste for evil, your instability. Tell Him how self-love makes you unjust to others, how vanity tempts you to be insincere, how pride hides you from yourself and from others. If you thus pour out all your weaknesses, needs, and troubles, there will be no lack of what to say. You will never exhaust the subject, for it is continually being renewed. People who have no secrets from each other never want for subjects of conversation. They do not weigh their words for there is nothing to be held back. Neither do they seek for something to say. They talk out of the abundance of their heart. Without consideration, they simply say just what they think. . . . Blessed are those who attain such familiar, unreserved communication with God.[2]

We too will experience the blessing of such communication with God if we strive in the power of the Holy Spirit to be honest in prayer. Tozer notes that "prayer will increase in power and reality as we repudiate all pretenses and learn to be utterly honest before God as well as before men." May we strive for such honestly in the days ahead so that we might know Him better!

REFLECT AND APPLY

1. In *Faith Beyond Reason*, Tozer wrote, "For the most part, we live in a land of lies and deception. There is a psychology of deceit and mistrust ground into us from our birth. But when we enter

the realm of the kingdom of God, the realm of faith, we find everything is different."[3] Thus, we have adopted the dishonest ways of this world. Even as true believers, we have subtly—sometimes unknown to us or sometimes because the majority of the believers we know are doing it—become dishonest. Such dishonesty pervades our speech, our thoughts, and our actions. The sadness is this track has entered our prayer life and our communion with God every day. Little steps in this direction of dishonesty lead to more dishonesty with ourselves, with others, and with God. Spend some time in reflection on the little steps of dishonesty and repent of them. Once identified, reflect on how these specks of dishonesty have affected your openness before the throne of grace and your ability to hear God's voice.

2. Is it possible that our greatest dishonesty is that we think our prayer life is okay, but in reality it is characterized with prayerlessness and the lack of power? Tozer says that "prayer will increase in power and in reality as we repudiate all pretense and learn to be utterly honest before God as well as before men." For the next week in the power of the Holy Spirit, ask God to help you be honest before Him and before men. After the week, reflect on your prayer times before the throne of grace.

3. Do you bring before the throne of grace your pleasures, your pains, your troubles, your vanities, your longings, your dislikes, your indifferences, your temptations, your wounds of the soul, your prideful perspectives, your depraved tastes, and

especially your weaknesses? Place the words of François Fénelon on a card or sheet of paper to be used as a bookmark for a month in your Bible to remind you what honesty in prayer should be like. For the next month, try to hit three of the items a week. For instance, Monday your pleasures, Wednesday your pains, and Saturday your troubles. Then the next week, focus on three different items. After the month is over, evaluate whether you sense a greater openness and honesty before God!

4. "The artless little child is still the divine model [for prayer] for all of us." This child has not been contaminated by the artificiality of civilized human beings, has not shown a concern for making good impressions, has not been affected by false and phony etiquette, and has not been biased by the religious jargon and attitudes of the day. How does one cultivate this model for prayer in our fast-paced society? Take a week and try to pray as a child. After that week, assess your honesty before God!

19

MEASURING SPIRITUALITY BY PUBLIC PRAYERS

The depths of a man's spirituality may be known quite accurately by the quality of his public prayers.

Bible prayers remain the most perfect examples of what prayer should be to most please our heavenly Father. How bold they are, yet how respectful; how intimate, yet how deeply reverent.

Those who heard Martin Luther's prayers have told us of the tremendous effect they often had upon the listeners. He would begin in moving humility, his spirit facedown in utter self-abnegation, and sometimes rise to a boldness of petition that would startle the hearers.

There is among us today a pseudo-mysticism that affects a tender intimacy with God but lacks that breathless awe which the true worshiper must always feel in the presence of the Holy God. This simpering spirit sometimes expresses itself in religious baby talk wholly unworthy of those who are addressing the Most High.

To hear a so-called Christian cooing in a voice indelicately familiar, addressing words of saccharine sweetness to one whom he or she calls "Jesus dear," is a shocking experience for anyone who has once seen heaven opened and stood speechless before the Holy Presence. No one who has ever bowed before the burning bush can thereafter speak lightly of God, much less be guilty of levity in addressing Him.

When Horace Bushnell prayed in the field under the night sky, his friend who knelt by his side drew in his arms close to his body. "I was afraid to stretch out my hands," he said, "lest I touch God."

While prayers are not addressed to the listeners, they are, nevertheless, meant to be heard by them and should be made with that knowledge frankly in mind. Paul makes this perfectly clear in his First Corinthian epistle. Finney had much to say about this also, as did certain others of the religious great.

We would do well in these days of superficialities in religion to rethink the whole matter of public prayer. It will lose nothing of spiritual content from being subjected to prayerful thought and reverent criticism.

From *The Early Tozer*
(1997; repr., Camp Hill, PA WingSpread, 2010)

EXPLORING WITH TOZER

The closest account of measuring the spirituality of prayers is given by Jesus in the parable of the Pharisee and the publican praying in the temple (Luke 18:9–14). The account is given below:

> And He also told this parable to some people who trusted in themselves that they were righteous, and viewed others with contempt: "Two men went up into the temple to pray, one a Pharisee and the other a tax collector. The Pharisee stood and was praying this to himself: 'God, I thank You that I am not like other people: swindlers, unjust, adulterers, or even like this tax collector. I fast twice a week; I pay tithes of all that I get.' But the tax collector, standing some distance away, was even unwilling to lift up his eyes to heaven, but was beating his breast, saying, 'God, be merciful to me, the sinner!' I tell you, this man went to his house justified rather than the other; for everyone who exalts himself will be humbled, but he who humbles himself will be exalted."

A quick comparison of the two men reveals their spirituality. The Pharisee prayed to self or for men, while the publican prayed to God. The Pharisee had words of thanksgiving but the tax collector had a heart filled with thanksgiving. The Pharisee compared himself to others and thought himself better than others, even the tax collector, while the publican made his comparison to God alone. The Pharisee was prideful while the publican was humble. Even worse was that the Pharisee boasted in the works of the flesh, but the tax collector displayed his faith in his prayer. The Pharisee had much knowledge of the law but no experience in doing it, just like many today who enjoy knowing God's will rather than doing it. Finally, the Pharisee had no petition in his prayer, but the publican's prayer had a petition for mercy from the God of all mercy and grace.

The prayer of the Pharisee might have impressed religious people but not God, since the man praying had an inflated sense of self, a deflated sense of God, and a distorted sense of values.[1] His entire prayer was "I" centered, not "God-centered."

It is evident that there is no magic formula in repeating the words of the tax collector's prayer, but the Lord is desirous of us having the "tax collector's heart, a heart sensitive to sin and totally dependent on God's grace." If that is how we pray in private, we will pray likewise in public.

REFLECT AND APPLY

1. "The depths of a man's spirituality may be known quite accurately by the quality of his public prayers." Not only is the spirituality revealed in public prayer but also in private prayer. Public prayer can be evaluated by those listening, but private prayer is another matter. In might be worthwhile to transcribe our daily prayer, once in a while, to see if it is "I" centered or "God-centered." Lay the prayer before the Lord and ask Him to search your heart and words of the prayer; or if you have a spiritual mentor, ask him for some reverent criticism.

2. Tozer rightly notes that the Bible prayers remain the most perfect examples of what prayer should be like. I have always found the prayers of Abraham, Moses, Elijah, Nehemiah, Daniel, Jesus, Paul, and many more extremely rich on how to pray as to content. Make it a point to study the prayer of one of these Old Testament saints, Jesus' teaching on prayer in the New Testament, Jesus' actual prayers in the Gospels, or the prayer content in the Epistles once every two months. Expect to come away from such a prayerful study with changes in how you pray! Record your findings in a prayer journal.

3. Public and private prayer should reflect a tender intimacy with God that is empowered by a daily walk with Christ in the power of the Holy Spirit. For instance, is your intimacy with God as rich as it was with Abraham and God as recorded in Genesis 18? How is such tender intimacy with God cultivated?

4. "We would do well in these days of superficialities in religion to rethink the whole matter of public prayer. It will lose nothing of spiritual content from being subjected to prayerful thought and reverent criticism." Evaluate this statement in your sphere of influence and in your church.

THE BEST THINGS
COME HARD

In this twisted world of ours the most important things are often the most difficult to learn; and conversely, the things that come easiest are mostly of little real value to us in the long haul.

This is seen clearly in the Christian life, where it often happens that the things we learn to do with the least trouble are the superficial and less important activities, and the really vital exercises tend to be avoided because of their difficulty.

It is seen still more clearly in our various forms of Christian service, particularly in the ministry. There the most difficult activities are the ones that produce the greatest fruit, and the less fruitful services are performed with the least effort. This constitutes a trap into which the wise minister will not fall, or if he should find that he is already caught in it he will assault heaven and earth in his determined fight to escape.

To pray successfully is the first lesson the preacher must learn if he is to preach fruitfully. Yet prayer is the hardest thing he will ever be called upon to do and, being human, it is the one act he will be tempted to do less frequently than any other. He must set his heart to conquer by prayer, and that will mean that he must first conquer his own flesh, for it is the flesh that hinders prayer always.

Almost anything associated with the ministry may be learned with an average amount of intelligent application. It is not hard to preach or manage church affairs or pay a social call; weddings and funerals may be conducted smoothly with a little help from Emily Post and the Minister's Manual. Sermon making can be learned as easily as shoemaking—introduction, conclusion and all. And so with the whole work of the ministry as it is carried on in the average church today.

But prayer—that is another matter. There Mrs. Post is helpless and the Minister's Manual can offer no assistance. There the lonely man of God must wrestle it out alone, sometimes in fastings and tears and weariness untold. There every man must be an original, for true prayer cannot be imitated nor can it be learned from someone else. Everyone must pray as if he alone could pray, and his approach must be individual and independent; independent, that is, of everyone but the Holy Spirit.

Thomas á Kempis says that the man of God ought to be more at home in his prayer chamber than before the public. It is not too much to say that the preacher who loves to be before the public is hardly prepared spiritually to be before them. Right praying may easily make a man hesitant to appear before an audience. The man who is really at home in the presence of God will find himself caught in a kind of inward contradiction. He is likely to feel his responsibility so keenly that he would rather do almost anything than face an audience; and yet the pressure upon his spirit may be so great that wild horses could not drag him away from his pulpit.

No man should stand before an audience who has not first stood before God. Many hours of communion should precede one hour in the pulpit. The prayer chamber should be more familiar than the public platform. Prayer should be continuous, preaching but intermittent.

It is significant that the schools teach everything about preaching except the important part, praying. For this weakness the schools are not to be blamed, for the reason that prayer cannot be taught; it can only be done. The best any school or any book (or any article) can do is to recommend prayer and exhort its practice. Praying itself must be the work of the individual. That it is the one religious work which gets done with the least enthusiasm cannot but be one of the tragedies of our times.

From *God Tells the Man Who Cares*

(1993; repr., Camp Hill, PA: WingSpread, 2010)

EXPLORING WITH TOZER

The Scriptures mention that Jesus not only taught on prayer but that He also considered prayer a critical spiritual discipline necessary to knowing and doing God's will every day. For instance, "In the early morning, while it was still dark, Jesus got up . . . and went away to a secluded place, and was praying there" (Mark 1:35). He prayed all night (Luke 6:12–13) prior to the selection of the twelve disciples, and in Luke 5:16 it is recorded that "Jesus Himself would often slip away to the wilderness and pray."

His life was permeated with prayer to the Father in key life moments, in the face of the deep needs of others, after rejection by men, at the Last Supper, in the garden of Gethsemane, and on the cross. He was always praying, with teaching on prayer sprinkled in His ministry.

However, it is interesting that while Jesus was praying at a certain place, one of the disciples approached Him and said, "Lord, teach us to pray just as John taught his disciples" (Luke 11:1). With all of the modeling and teaching on prayer, the disciples still felt very inadequate and ill-equipped in prayer. It is very possible that the recent failure on the Mount of Transfiguration by the three disciples [Peter, James, and John], who were sleeping, and in the valley by the other nine disciples, who were powerless to cast the demon out of a father's only son, triggered this question of how to pray. In the latter scenario, Jesus' response was that "this kind cannot come out by anything but prayer" (Mark 9:29). If there is little faith, there is little prayer; on the other hand, when there is genuine, persevering faith in God and His Word, there is fervent, unrelenting prayer.

It takes prayer to see the degree of demoniac difficulties, the levels of pain, the destructive intensities of bondage, and the extent of the deception. Once this is seen from God's perspective, then God's unique solution for the case must be applied. The disciples were evidently looking for a magic formula for prayer and success in life and ministry, and there is really none.

Tozer captures the reality of this query by the disciples when he notes "that prayer cannot be taught; it can only be done." We have a strong tendency to rely on methods and skills which have served us well in the past instead of prayer. Many of the difficulties, trials, or problems that come our way may seem simple but in reality they are quite complex. As noted in *A Mosaic of Faith,*

> If the problem is extremely difficult, one needs divine insight and discernment along with the Word of God to pray about the different parts of the problem (the seen and the unseen) and to know God's timeline about how to proceed.
>
> There is nothing too little to bring up before the Lord. Zechariah 4:10 says, "For who has despised the day of small things?"—no matter whether the smallness is related to the type of problem or the small parts of a very complex problem.
>
> Praying this way is a spiritual discipline that is ingrained into the life along with a continual dependence upon Christ, His Spirit, and the sword of the Spirit. One of the reasons this kind of praying is not ingrained into many believers' lives is that we see our problems as one-dimensional and not multifaceted with many unseen problems or subissues.[1]

Such ingraining takes practice under the daily tutelage of the Holy Spirit. In addition, the believer cannot survive on baby food for the prayer battles of tomorrow since baby food does not prepare the heart or mind to discern between good and evil (Heb. 5:14). He must "grow in the grace and knowledge of our Lord and Savior Jesus Christ" (2 Peter 3:18). Solid biblical teaching in the power of the Holy Spirit from the pulpit as well as our own searching of the Scriptures daily (Acts 17:11) will greatly aid this growth in grace and knowledge to expand our prayer effectiveness. We must be careful that we don't assess this effectiveness purely from our perspective but from God's perspective—mainly in that He is glorified.

REFLECT AND APPLY

1. "To pray successfully is the first lesson the preacher must learn if he is to preach fruitfully; yet prayer is the hardest thing he will ever be called upon to do and, being human, it is the one act he will be tempted to do less frequently than any other." This statement of Tozer is dripping with deep truths. For the preacher, fruitfulness in preaching is linked to successful praying. But cannot the same correlation be made for the layman that his fruitfulness in his ministry, job, and family is tied to his success in praying? Ask yourself honestly whether you have a biblical schedule that allows you to linger before the Lord and pray as Abraham (Gen. 18) or Joshua (Ex. 33:7–11) did. Assess your frequency of prayer. What answers would you give for little or no praying today? Pray about the changes that God would have you make to return to your first love!

2. Tozer said that a man "must set his heart to conquer by prayer, and that will mean that he must

156

first conquer his own flesh for it is the flesh that hinders prayer always." Reflect on this statement.

3. "The lonely man of God must wrestle it out alone, sometimes in fastings and tears and weariness untold. There every man must be an original, for true prayer cannot be imitated nor can it be learned from someone else. Everyone must pray as if he alone could pray, and his approach must be individual and independent; independent, that is, of everyone but the Holy Spirit." In light of Tozer's comment here, where do group praying, reading books on prayer, studying the prayers of the Old and New Testament saints, and analyzing biblical texts on prayer fit in? Again, honestly ask yourself under the scrutiny of the Holy Spirit about whether you have had these wrestlings or this journey in prayer over the past twelve months. If not, ask God to sanctify your prayer times in the days ahead. If so, ask God to gently move you to the next level of praying.

4. "Prayer cannot be taught; it can only be done. The best any school or any book (or any article) can do is to recommend prayer and exhort its practice. Praying itself must be the work of the individual. That it is the one religious work which gets done with the least enthusiasm cannot but be one of the tragedies of our time." Assuredly, we should agree that there is little enthusiasm about praying today, even though sermons, books, and the like do exhort us to pray. Is it possible these exhortations to pray do not change our heart and motivations to pray because they are secondhand? Yet we may have come across a need for which there

is no solution but God's in His time. We may well need firsthand, in-depth time in the Word of God to understand our God, His ways, and His priorities. Study the prayers of Abraham, Moses, Daniel, and more for a few months and see the sanctification of your prayer time and the new directions of your prayers.

5. "Thomas á Kempis says that the man of God ought to be more at home in his prayer chamber than before the public." Do you feel likewise in your prayer chamber than before people at work, in your community, in your political arena, in your ministry, and in your family? Ask God to help you feel more at home in prayer over the next thirty days. If that does occur, what differences do you expect to see?

A WORD TO THE MEN ABOUT THE WOMEN

Prayer is not a work that can be allocated to one or another group in the church. It is everybody's responsibility; it is everybody's privilege. Prayer is the respiratory function of the church; without it we suffocate and die at last, like a living body deprived of the breath of life. Prayer knows no gender, for the soul has no sex, and it is the soul that must pray. Women can pray, and their prayers will be answered; but so can men, and so should men if they are to fill the place God has given them in the church.

Let us watch that we do not slide imperceptibly to a state where the women do the praying and the men run the churches. Men who do not pray have no right to direct church affairs. We believe in the leadership of men within the spiritual community of the saints, but that leadership should be won by spiritual worth.

Leadership requires vision, and whence will vision come except from hours spent in the presence of God in humble and fervent prayer? All things else being equal, a praying woman will know the will of God for the church far better than a prayerless man.

We do not here advocate the turning of the churches over to the women, but we do advocate a recognition of proper spiritual qualifications for leadership among the men if they are to continue to decide the direction the churches shall take. The accident of being a man is not enough. Spiritual manhood alone qualifies.

"Look ye out among you seven men of honest report," commanded the apostles, "full of the Holy Ghost and wisdom, whom we may appoint over this business" (Acts 6:3). The men chosen as a consequence of this directive became the first deacons of the church. Thus the direction of certain church affairs was put into the hands of men spiritually qualified. Should we not maintain the same standards today?

We Travel an Appointed Way, rev. ed.

(1988; repr., Camp Hill, PA: WingSpread, 2010)

EXPLORING WITH TOZER

Tozer's words about prayer in this section reflect what he was seeing in the church during his day, the women praying much more than the men. If we would step back and be honest before God, the situation today is about the same in some churches but worst in most since there is little prayer by either gender. Romans 12:12 tells us that all believers should be "devoted to prayer," and Jude 1:20 encourages believers to build "yourselves up on your most holy faith, praying in the Holy Spirit." Building ourselves up in our most holy faith requires the Word of God (a listening to God), obedience to the Word in the power of the Holy Spirit (a righteous doing before God), and prayer to God (a daily conversation with God). In essence, every believer is exhorted to be devoted to prayer, but it must be prayer empowered or enabled by the Holy Spirit as well as grounded in the Word of God.

The apostle Paul reminds us of the spiritual battle going on around us all of the time: "Finally, be strong in the Lord and in the strength of His might. Put on the full armor of God, so that you will be able to stand firm against the schemes of the devil . . . With all prayer and petition pray at all times in the Spirit, and with this in view, be on the alert with all perseverance and petition for all the saints" (Eph. 6:10–11, 18).

His reminder should prick our souls that the Bible is the real world. Tozer himself has noted that many saints see this world as a playground, not a battleground, and thus are frolicking instead of fighting. The end result is that they don't see the value of prayer to God, for the church, for their own family, and for impacting their world for Christ. This prayerlessness that we see in the church among men or women is evidence of our barrenness in the Word of God and in walking by faith. E. M. Bounds made the following comment about prayer:

What the Church needs today is not more machinery or better, not new organizations or more and novel methods, but men whom the Holy Ghost can use—men of prayer, men mighty in prayer. The Holy Ghost does not flow through methods, but through men. He does not anoint plans, but men—men of prayer.[1]

Sad to say then, we are seeing an increasing trust in methods, machinery, and strategies instead of a greater trust in and dependence on God alone. How do we change the trend? We must "humble ourselves under the mighty hand of God" (1 Peter 5:6) as we permanently adopt His ways and His priorities. This holds for men and women if we are truly to be God's people of light and salt in this fallen world.

REFLECT AND APPLY

1. "Prayer is not a work that can be allocated to one or another group in the church. It is everybody's responsibility; it is everyone's privilege. Prayer is the respiratory function of the church; without it we suffocate and die at last, like a living body deprived of the breadth of life." Reflect on this statement and ask God to enable you to honestly assess it in your church and your circumstances. Or better yet, personalize it by asking yourself whether there are people you run to for prayer support when strange things happen. Do you likewise keep praying or do you shift the responsibility totally to others? What would God have you change in your prayer life in this situation?

2. "Let us watch that we do not slide imperceptibly to a state where the women do the praying and the men run the churches. Men who do not pray have no right to direct church affairs." It is easy to slide, unknowingly, to a place where prayer is not the priority of all in the church but a select few. What is the priority of prayer in your church or in your life? Are the leaders in your church or ministry known for being people of prayer? Has there been an imperceptible slide on the importance and practice of prayer in your Christian community? What must be done to turn the tide? Spend some time praying about this turning of the tide by men and women.

3. "Leadership requires vision, and whence will vision come except from hours spent in the presence of God in humble and fervent prayer?" Meditate on this statement.

4. Tozer rightly advocates the recognition of "proper spiritual qualifications for leadership among the men if they are to continue to decide the direction the churches shall take." So many times when leaders are chosen in a local church, there are no questions about the commitment to prayer for the candidate leader. The apostles had the right commitment as evidenced by Acts 6:4: "But we will devote ourselves to prayer and to the ministry of the word." Honestly ask yourself if prayer has had that priority in your life and ministry. What would you say to a young believer who was struggling with this priority of prayer or to a candidate for church leadership that did not have this priority?

DOES GOD ALWAYS
ANSWER PRAYER?

Contrary to popular opinion, the cultivation of a psychology of uncritical belief is not an unqualified good, and if carried too far it may be a positive evil. The whole world has been booby-trapped by the devil, and the deadliest trap of all is the religious one. Error never looks so innocent as when it is found in the sanctuary.

One field where harmless looking but deadly traps appear in great profusion is the field of prayer. There are more sweet notions about prayer than could be contained in a large book, all of them wrong and all highly injurious to the souls of men.

I think of one such false notion that is found often in pleasant places consorting smilingly with other notions of unquestionable orthodoxy. It is that *God always answers prayer.*

This error appears among the saints as a kind of all-purpose philosophic therapy to prevent any disappointed Christian from suffering too great a shock when it becomes evident to him that his prayer expectations are not being fulfilled. It is explained that God always answers prayer, either by saying yes or by saying no, or by substituting something else for the desired favor.

Now, it would be hard to invent a neater trick than this to save face for the petitioner whose requests have been rejected for non-obedience. Thus when a prayer is not answered he has but to smile brightly and explain, "God said no." It is all so very comfortable. His wobbly faith is saved from confusion and his conscience is permitted to lie undisturbed. But I wonder if it is honest.

To receive an answer to prayer as the Bible uses the term and as Christians have understood it historically, two elements must be present: (1) A clear-cut request made to God for a specific favor. (2) A clear-cut granting of that favor by God in answer to the request. There must be no semantic twisting, no changing of labels, no altering of the map during the journey to help the embarrassed tourist to find himself.

When we go to God with a request that He modify the existing situation for us, that is, that He answer prayer, there are two conditions that we must meet: (1) We must pray in the will of God. (2) We must be on what old-fashioned Christians often call "praying ground"; that is, we must be living lives pleasing to God.

It is futile to beg God to act contrary to His revealed purposes. To pray with confidence the petitioner must be certain that his request falls within the broad will of God for His people.

The second condition is also vitally important. God has not placed Himself under obligation to honor the requests of worldly, carnal, or disobedient Christians. He hears and answers the prayers only of those who walk in His way:

Beloved, if our heart condemn us not, then have we confidence toward God. And whatsoever we ask, we receive of him, because we keep his commandments, and do those things that are pleasing in his sight. . . . If ye abide in me, and my words abide in you, ye shall ask what ye will, and it shall be done unto you. (1 John 3:21–22; John 15:7)

God wants us to pray and He wants to answer our prayers, but He makes our use of prayer as a privilege to commingle with His use of prayer as a discipline. To receive answers to prayer we must meet God's terms. If we neglect His commandments our petitions will not be honored. He will alter situations only at the request of obedient and humble souls.

The God-always-answers-prayer sophistry leaves the praying man without discipline. By the exercise of this bit of smooth casuistry, he ignores the necessity to live soberly, righteously, and godly in this present world, and actually takes God's flat refusal to answer his prayer as the very answer itself. Of course such a man will not grow in holiness; he will never learn how to wrestle and wait; he will never know correction; he will not hear the voice of God calling him forward; he will never arrive at the place where he is morally and spiritually fit to have his prayers answered. His wrong philosophy has ruined him.

That is why I turn aside to expose the bit of bad theology upon which his bad philosophy is founded. The man who accepts it never knows where he stands; he never knows whether or not he has true faith, for if his request is not granted he avoids the implication by the simple dodge of declaring that God switched the whole thing around and gave him something else. He will not allow himself to shoot at a target, so he cannot tell how good or how bad a marksman he is.

Of certain persons James says plainly: "Ye ask, and receive not, because ye ask amiss, that ye may consume it upon your lusts" (4:3). From that brief sentence we may learn that God refuses some requests because they who make them are not morally worthy to receive the answer. But this means nothing to the one who has been seduced into the belief that God always answers prayer. When such a man asks and receives not, he passes his hand over the hat and comes up with the answer in some other form. One thing he clings to with great tenacity: God never turns anyone away, but invariably grants every request.

The truth is that God always answers the prayer that accords with His will as revealed in the Scriptures, provided the one who prays is obedient and trustful. Further than this we dare not go.

From *Man: The Dwelling Place of God*
(1966; repr., Camp Hill, PA: WingSpread, 2006)

EXPLORING WITH TOZER

Do you not know that friendship with the world is hostility toward God? Therefore whoever wishes to be a friend of the world makes himself an enemy of God" (James 4:4). Such a friendship with the world means not thinking God's thoughts, not obeying God's Word, not praying in God's will, and not pursuing God's will be done but one's own will in personal affairs. As a friend of the world, the worldly believer can be easily deceived into thinking that God always answers prayer without any divine searching of his own heart when the answer is no. However, the friend of God, as Abraham was called and as Jesus' disciples were referenced (John 15:14–15), could handle a yes, a no, or a petition change. Such friends were on "praying ground" as they had lives that were pleasing to the Father.

We are not on "praying ground" when sins' long tentacles have reached into our lives, or when we have conformed to the world. God's will is that we do not continually practice sin. If we do sin—and we all do (1 John 1:8–9)—we confess it and accept God's forgiveness and cleansing; then we move forward in the power of the Holy Spirit. When involved in sin, God will hear our prayer; but the answer will be no. (Now, there can be other reasons for a no answer, such as not now.)

Further, every believer should know that God can never answer prayers that are against His will. What is God's will for us? For sure, it is to be holy in all that we do and think, to serve Him in purity and to not serve ourselves, to be light in the midst of darkness, and to make disciples in Christ.

One way to assess this praying ground is to look at our requests to God the Father. For instance, how many of our prayer requests are just to keep up with the "Joneses?" Or how many of our requests are to maintain appearances, to keep us comfortable in our sphere of life, to give us an advantage over someone else, or maybe to give us a boast before others? This underlying friendship with the world undermines our relationship with our Almighty God, weakens our prayer life, and leaves us devoid of discernment.

Hebrews 5:14 says, "but solid food is for the mature, who because of practice have their senses trained to discern good and evil." Let us back track this verse. First, there is a lack of discernment both in the Christian walk but even moreso in prayer. Note what Tozer says about the lack of spiritual discernment from *The Root of the Righteous*:

> The great deficiency to which I refer is the lack of spiritual discernment, especially among our leaders. How there can be so much Bible knowledge and so little insight, so little moral penetration, is one of the enigmas of the religious world today. . . . If the knowledge of Bible doctrine were any guarantee of godliness, this would without doubt be known in history as the age of sanctity. Instead, it may well be known as the age of the Church's Babylonish captivity, or the age of worldliness, when the professed Bride of Christ allowed herself to be successfully courted by the fallen sons of men in unbelievable numbers.[1]

Second, this lack of discernment tracks back to not having our spiritual senses trained by the practice of the Word of God. It is possible that a believer has only head knowledge, or gives just mental agreement to the Word but never takes the time to meditate on it and let it become part of their inner life—or has not bowed the knee to the truth revealed. Jesus warned His followers, "Take care how you listen; for whoever has, to him more shall be given; and whoever does not have, even what he thinks he has shall be taken away" (Luke 8:18). Thus, our listening to the Word and applying it to our life is critical in being discerning, even in prayer. Third, solid food from the Word of God is necessary for this discernment. The words of Paul in 1 Corinthians 3:1–3 capture this importance:

> And I, brethren, could not speak to you as to spiritual men, but as to men of flesh, as to infants in Christ. I gave you milk to drink, not solid food; for you were not yet able to receive it. Indeed, even now you are not yet able, for you are still fleshly. For since there is jealousy and strife among you, are you not fleshly, and are you not walking like mere men?

Solid food from the Scriptures, accompanied by the empowerment and the work of the Holy Spirit in the believer's life, makes that biblical truth real. However, many believers are not hungering for solid food; they are satisfied with milk and learning the elementary principles of the Word over and over (Heb. 5:11–13), and they have accumulated teachers who tickle their ears and cater to their own desires (2 Tim. 4:3). The end result is a friendship with the world that is hostility toward God as evidenced by the inability to discern that the answer to the believer's prayer is "no" because of his non-obedience.

We are supposed to be "a fragrance of Christ to God" (2 Cor. 2:15), not walking like the natural man and being a stench to the Father because of our worldiness. Our prayers should be sweet incense before the throne. May we strive for such in the power of the Holy Spirit as we ask Him to aid us in rightly discerning the answers to our prayers!

REFLECT AND APPLY

1. "One field where harmless looking but deadly traps appear in great profusion is the field of prayer. There are more sweet notions about prayer than could be contained in a large book, all of them wrong and all highly injurious to the souls of men." One of these is that "God always answered prayer." Some aspects of the injuries to the soul are (1) the failure of the believer to ask God the Holy Spirit to search his heart and expose the worldliness or ungodly perspectives that hinder the answered prayer, (2) a diminished hunger for the meat of the Word, (3) a growing lack of discernment between good and evil, (4) a decline in discipline and persistence in the things of God, (5) lack of growth in holiness, (6) and a strong tendency to conform more and more to the world. Reflect on some prayers that you received an answer of no to over the past year. What was your response to those no answers? Were they monumental moments that moved you to excel still more in Christ, or did you rationalize away the answer and stay where you were spiritually (or even took steps backward in your life)? Spend some time during the next week reflecting on this question.

2. "The God-always-answers-prayer sophistry leaves the praying man without discipline. By the exercise of this bit of smooth casuistry he ignores the necessity to live soberly, righteously, and godly in this present world, and actually takes God's flat refusal to answer his prayer as the very answer itself. Of course such a man will not grow in holiness; he

will never learn how to wrestle and wait; he will never know correction; he will not hear the voice of God calling him forward; he will never arrive at the place where he is morally and spiritually fit to have his prayers answered. His wrong philosophy has ruined him." Thus, a lack of growth in holiness, a shortage of desire to wrestle and wait for God, an unwillingness to receive correction, and/or an inability to hear the voice of God are all signs of non-obedience that has corrupted our prayer life and our communion with the Father on a daily basis. Spend some time reflecting on whether some of these signs have showed up in your life in Christ. If the signs reflect lukewarmness about your spiritual disciplines and the things of God, repent quickly and seek first the kingdom of God.

3. "God has not placed Himself under obligation to honor the requests of worldly, carnal or disobedient Christians. He hears and answers the prayers only of those who walk in His way." If we can be easily deceived by our disobedience as to the answers to our prayers, maybe it would be helpful to keep a prayer diary to track our prayers and the answers. (One must be careful that this prayer diary does not become a means to boast to others about our prayer prominence.) In addition, we need more mature believers who can mentor us, who can speak into our lives with correction and encouragement, and who can model being "holy in all your behavior" (1 Peter 1:15). Who is or are your mentors in Christ? If none, begin praying about God providing at least one.

4. "God wants us to pray and He wants to answer our prayers, but He makes our use of prayer as a privilege to commingle with His use of prayer as a discipline." Tozer has succinctly captured God's desire for communion with Him and His desire to change or impact our sphere of influence in this fallen world through prayer. Personally, I'm concerned that my prayerlessness at times as a result of my own sin or busyness or poor priorities could nix God's best in some situations, but the big loser is that I have missed being a colaborer with the infinite and almighty God of the universe. May we sense this loss and ever be empowered by the Holy Spirit to keep praying.

23

VAGUE PRAYING AND EXPECTATION

Praying is God's method of getting things done on earth. Jesus said, "All things are possible to him who believes," and also said, "For all things are possible with God" (Mark 9:23b; 10:27b). Prayer unites God and the praying man in one and says God is omnipotent and the praying man is omnipotent (for the time being), because he is in touch with omnipotence.

I see an awful lot of unbelieving humility and constant self-reproach—apologetic, timid and afraid. We dare not be. "Let us draw near with confidence to the throne of grace, so that we may receive mercy and find grace to help in time of need" (Heb. 4:16). So let's come boldly. Shouldn't we be humble? Certainly we should. But no man should be so humble that he doesn't ask, or we're playing into the hands of the devil. We should be humble, but we should dare to ask and seek and knock.

There must be expectation. We've got to point up our prayers. I have said it before and repeat it, that one of the greatest snares in praying is to pray vaguely. I used to go out rifle shooting in the state of Pennsylvania. I still like to when I get out that way. I used to enjoy using a big gun, like an eight millimeter or a 30–30, because the thing would go "Boom!" and the smoke would fly and I'd almost fall over and I felt really big. But if I'd been shooting at something, I was red-faced because I'd usually miss it.

And when a man prays vaguely, he makes a big boom and others say, "Oh, he is a praying man." But what is he praying about? Has God heard his prayer, or is he just shooting at a cloud? How do you know if he hits it? He is shooting at the side of a barn. Maybe he hit it or maybe that's just a knothole you see there. Shoot at a definite target and if you miss, say, "No, I didn't hit it. I'm sorry." If I pray for something and God doesn't give it, it doesn't do God any honor for me to make myself believe I have it.

You want to be filled with the Holy Spirit, and you say, "All right now, I'll take it." That's what you think. You ought to be willing to let God test you and know whether He's answered your prayer or not. Well, you've got to expect.

Edited sermon, Southwest Alliance Church, Chicago; no date[1]

EXPLORING WITH TOZER

This short piece on prayer is power packed with the ingredients for successful praying: boldness, humility, a need, faith, expectation, and specific requests. However, the emphasis is on a specific or definite request (generated by a need) clothed in humility, undergirded in faith and expectation, but boldly expressed in light of God's Word. Andrew Murray said it well:

> Our prayers must not be a vague appeal to His mercy, an indefinite cry for blessing, but the distinct expression of definite need. Not that His loving heart does not understand our cry, or is not ready to hear. But He desires it for our own sakes. Such definite prayer teaches us to know our own needs better. It demands time, and thought, and self-scrutiny to find out what really is our greatest need. It searches us and puts us to the test as to whether our desires are honest and real, such as we are ready to persevere in. It leads us to judge whether our desires are according to God's Word, and whether we really believe that we shall receive the things we ask. It helps us to wait for the special answer, and to mark it when it comes.[2]

Such a specific or definite prayer has many advantages. First, we must know our needs better to formulate such a specific request. That requires time before the Lord so that He can shape the request to be specific; but our hustle and bustle lifestyle does not provide time to sit simply, honestly, and quietly before the Lord. The not-so-good result of vague praying is the lack of knowing our Savior and God specifically better. Second, our prayer journey with a specific request is a true barometer of our growing or stagnant faith. For instance, do we persevere with the specific request but allow God to reshape certain details of the request over time? Or do we start out praying a specific request but grow weary in waiting for God's answer in His time or get upset when He doesn't answer it our way?

We must never forget that delays in answers to prayer are part of God's divine purpose. He uses those divine delays sometimes to reshape and make our prayers more specific. When a Syrophoenician woman, a Gentile, came to Jesus (Matt. 15:21–28), continually asking Him to cast the demon out of her daughter, she based her request on Jesus being the Son of David. Yet the Scriptures record that "He did not answer her a word" (v. 23). The grounds of her request were not biblically correct—He was the Son of David to Israel, not the Gentiles. The woman asked again. "Lord, help me!" Jesus' reply was "it is not good to take the children's bread and throw it to the dogs" (Matt. 15:26). The woman persevered in her request and reshaped it in light of Jesus' words that "even the dogs feed on the crumbs which fall from their masters' table" (Matt. 15:26). The result of her perseverance with a specific biblically reshaped request was the answer she sought, but also a commendation that her faith was great (v. 28).

Her journey in this specific request revealed great faith in God and a much closer relationship with Him. May we likewise pursue our Savior with God's enabling power for answers to our specific requests while clothed with humility and standing on the Word of God. In that way, His name is glorified and lifted up!

REFLECT AND APPLY

1. Consider the depths of Tozer's statement: "Prayer unites God and the praying man in one and says God is omnipotent and the praying man is omnipotent (for the time being)." Is not this ability

to interface with the omnipotent One due to the Christian praying according to God's will for an individual or specific situation? Does not such a reality empower our praying, make us more conscious of praying according to God's will, and free us to seek His face in all? Ask yourself these questions and contemplate the truth of Tozer's statement for the next week.

2. Vague praying does not allow us to know if we have received that which we have asked of God. Such praying can undermine our faith. For sure, we sometimes start out praying vaguely for something; but if we are really seeking God's will in prayer, will not God reshape that prayer? Reflect back over the past six months of some prayers that were vague. Did you keep praying that way, did you drop the request, or did God make the request more specific? It is important for each of us at times to take inventory of the nature of our past prayers so that we can grow in grace, in knowledge, and in maturity in Christ.

3. At times a busy lifestyle can rob us of time to sit simply and quietly before the Lord in prayer and in the study of God's Word. If that could be the case for you, it could be one explanation for vague, rut-like prayers. What are some other explanations for vague praying instead of definite prayers in your life?

4. Delays to prayers being answered are divine! The prayer might be not according to His will at the time, the prayer might be not standing on the appropriate Scripture, the delay could be testing

our perseverance and faith, or the prayer could need re-shaping so that we will recognize the answer when it comes resulting in our faith growing in leaps and bounds. Spend fifteen minutes each week for the next month reflecting on the delays you have experienced and the results you received. Give thanks to God for those delays and what you learned in them.

24

IN EVERYTHING BY PRAYER

I have noticed in recent years that all of the Lord's people—not just ministers and missionaries—tend more and more to become a nervous and harried people. Paul wrote to the Philippians and said, "Be anxious for nothing. . . . And the peace of God will guard your hearts and your minds" (Phil. 4:6–7 all NASB).

It is natural that people will have fears and concerns about their families, about their safety and about their health. God has said that we don't know what will be on the morrow. Mostly these fears are driven inward and underground into what they call the subconscious—that which worries underneath. It's the thing you dream with, and the thing you worry with when you don't know you are worrying.

The result of that is, of course, that it weakens, panics us, makes us nervous, and inclines to steal away our joy. Well, what are we going to do about it? Are we going to listen to the "don't worry" cult that says there's nothing in the wide world for you to be afraid of? Now, I know better than that. I'm not going to rest my nerves at the expense of my head—that is, I'm not going to commit intellectual suicide and listen to some tabby cat telling me there isn't anything to be afraid of in the world.

How are we going to escape fear, when there are legitimate dangers that lie all around us?

Well, here's what the man of God says: "Be anxious for nothing, but in everything by prayer and supplication with thanksgiving let your requests be made known to God. And the peace of God, which surpasses all comprehension, will guard your hearts and your minds in Christ Jesus" (Phil. 4:6–7).

Someone is looking after us. The Bible says "He cares for you" (1 Peter 5:7). Jesus, our Lord, says: "Your Father knows what you need before you ask Him" (Matt. 6:8). And Jesus said, "Do not let your heart be troubled" (John 14:1). And in all your afflictions, remember that He was afflicted, too.

The Bible pictures God as a very careful, tenderhearted Father, busying Himself about the troubles of His people. He looks after them, goes ahead of them, cares for them, and guides them all the way through. There you see the problem of worry and anxiety is solved by the assurance that while there are things about which to be concerned, why should you worry, when Somebody is taking care of you!

But now I just want to ask whether you are willing to let God take over? Remember that peace of heart does not come from denying that there is trouble, but comes from rolling your trouble on God. By faith you have the right to call on One who is your brother, the Son of Man who was also the Son of God. And if He's going to look after you, why should you worry at all!

Edited sermon; location and date not provided[1]

EXPLORING WITH TOZER

This call to escape anxious feelings and instead surrender to God—giving thanks in prayer for everything He sends your way— is among only a couple references to Philippians 4:6–7 in Tozer's writings. In addition to this short one from *The Tozer Pulpit* there is a sermon by Tozer entitled "In Everything by Prayer."[2] That sermon is unique in that Tozer addressed most of the replacement options for "in everything by prayer: in everything by money, in everything by social prestige, in everything by publicity, in everything by committee, in everything by business methods, in everything by education, and lastly in everything by compromise. All of these replacement options are found wanting in the eyes of God, yet Christians continue to regress to them.

Of these eight options, not one pleases God, and each of them adds to the stress and anxiety of life.

We are all guilty of slipping into these options of money, prestige, publicity, committee, business, education, and compromise at some time in our Christian walk, most likely to obtain quick success. Instead, the Scriptures tell us the solution to anxiety is in everything that concerns us "by prayer and supplication with thanksgiving let your requests be made known to God."

Great leaders of ancient Israel struggled with this truth. Remember that Moses, in his frustration and anger with God's people (Numbers 20), didn't speak to the rock (as God commanded) but struck it. He got results of water for God's people and animals, but it was not God's way. He got quick success, but his ultimate consequence was not being able to go into the Promised Land. Joshua, a mighty warrior, agreed with the men of Israel based on the appearances of the age of clothing and food that the Gibeonites, asking for assistance, were telling the truth about their plight. However, the Scriptures record their telltale failure: they "did not ask for the counsel of the Lord" (Josh. 9:14). Here Joshua, Moses' disciple, did not bathe the decision in prayer but depended upon appearances. Then, there is David in 2 Samuel 24, who possibly in his pride sought to number the people against the counsel of his commander Joab. He did not pray, and again there were consequences.

The bottom line is that Moses, Joshua, and David were godly men who didn't do everything in prayer, and they experienced the consequences. Thus, we are in an elite company when we choose to make decisions not through prayer but our own, mind, or might. When we make decisions without coming first and last to God, we can be sure that there are consequences—and the most damaging consequences are damage to our faith, our future obedience, our relationship to our Savior and Lord, and to the name and glory of our God before believers and nonbelievers. Let us be diligent to pursue "in everything by prayer."

REFLECT AND APPLY

1. The command from Scripture is clear: "Be anxious for nothing, but in everything by prayer." Are the anxieties and fears, both conscious and subconscious, present in our lives because we have failed to be in prayer about everything and relied on other options of the flesh to secure a satisfactory or speedy conclusion? Sometimes, people start out praying; but when God delays His answer or moves toward an answer they don't want, they become anxious and fearful and look for other ways to manipulate our fleshy solution. How does one avoid responding to anxieties and fears without prayer? Will a mentor help? Will a stronger faith in Christ help? The next time a specific anxiety or fear occurs pray about it immediately and find Scripture to stand on for that request.

2. Tozer notes that the "peace of heart does not come from denying that there is trouble, but comes from rolling your trouble on God." There is a two-step progression here: (1) recognize that there is a problem or trouble that only God can handle. (We tend to categorize these troubles into those we can handle and those that God should handle.); and (2) roll the trouble or problem onto God since He cares for us. We tend to roll it to God but quickly pick it up in times of stress. Thus, we may need to keep rolling the trouble onto God repeatedly. In time, our faith will grow and the rolling onto God for the same problem will not be so frequent. What have you rolled onto Him lately? Did you pick it up again and have to recast your burden on Him? Honestly,

evaluate your willingness to cast your burdens on the Lord over the past two weeks.

3. Worry or anxiety "weakens, panics us, makes us nervous, and inclines to steal away our joy." Can you remember some specific times or events where your joy was robbed by worry? What was the essence of your praying during those times or events? Of course, people, circumstances, and things can also rob us of our joy. How should we respond to these thieves of our joy? Is it not "in everything by prayer?" One must be careful that anxiety can also hinder or thwart us in praying according to God's will. What steps do you need to take to avoid your joy in the Lord being stolen in the future or more specifically next week?

4. "The Bible pictures God as a very careful, tender-hearted Father, busying Himself about the troubles of His people. He looks after them . . . and guides them all the way through. There you see the problem of worry and anxiety is solved by the assurance that while there are things about which to be concerned, why should you worry, when Somebody is taking care of you!" Thus, our worry defames the character of God. For instance, we are fighting the sovereignty of God, doubting His omnipotence and love, and are being unwilling to rest in His mercies and faithfulness each day. Clearly worry is a sin that must be confessed. Once this sin is confessed, the filling of His Holy Spirit and our reliance on the Scriptures will give us an awesome view of God. Pray (again, in everything by prayer) that God will sensitize you to worry in your life.

JESUS LIVES TO MAKE INTERCESSION FOR US

At the risk of repeating a religious cliché, I must point out that the will of God is always best, whatever the circumstances. Jesus refused the crown and deliberately took the cross because the cross was in the will of God, both for Him and for humankind.

Let us not be afraid to take that cross ourselves and trust God to provide the crown in His own time. Why should so many in our day try to short-circuit their spiritual lives by eliminating the cross in route to the crown?

Our Lord took the Father's will. He refused the crown that Israel wanted to give Him and instead took the cross the Romans gave him. On the third day He arose from the dead. Forty days later, He ascended to His Father's right hand, His disciples seeing Him go. And there He is today!

In John 6, what did Jesus do when He went to the mountain alone (v.15)? He prayed. Jesus, that praying Man of all praying men, was talking to His heavenly Father. He was talking to Him about the little group of disciples whom He had just parted from a short time before—and about the five thousand people who had just been fed and in their ignorance wanted to make Him their king.

By the human reckoning of the multitude, Jesus would bring about a revolution that would set Israel free, as in the days of Gideon and the great judges and prophets of the Old Testament. But Jesus knew these people well. He knew the worst thing He could do would be to put on a crown and bring that carnal multitude into an earthly kingdom.

Actually, there would have to be many changes among them before they dared become sons and daughters of an earthly kingdom. So He was praying for them in their ignorance and in their confusion, praying to the heavenly Father for His sheep. *And that is exactly what He is doing now!* Jesus is in heaven, praying for His people. I do not mean that our Lord is on His knees continually in the glory land yonder, but He is in continual communion with the Father. "Wherefore he is able also to save them to the uttermost that come unto God by him, seeing he ever liveth to make intercession for them" (Heb. 7:25).

Edited sermon, Southwest Alliance Church,
Chicago; no date[1]

EXPLORING WITH TOZER

There are two "always" mentioned in this Tozer section. First, as illustrated by Jesus' example, He always wanted the will of the Father in His life. His desire for that will is displayed in His prayer in the garden of Gethsemane when He said the following: "Abba! Father! All things are possible for You; remove this cup from Me; yet not what I will, but what You will" (Mark 14:36).

There are two aspects of this specific prayer. One is that the cup could not be removed; or saying it more bluntly, this prayer could not be answered. The next part of this prayer is a prayer of submission to the will of God, which would be answered.

In essence, Jesus endured the non-answering of His prayer that our prayers might find an answer today and tomorrow. In other words, Jesus' submission to the best of God's will led to the best for us. Praise God for the wisdom of His will!

God's will is always best for us today just as it was for Jesus. However, many believers do not know His will as revealed in the Scriptures, they may ignore the biblical counseling that was received, or they may chaff at perceived restrictions that Scriptures bring on their life. Of course, such responses are typical of lives that are caught up in sin or that are immature in Christ. The great disadvantage is that these individuals are not on praying ground, and do not see God's will as best for them.

The next "always" is that Jesus "always lives to make intercession" (Heb.7:25) for us. Jesus is still praying for His sheep just as He did when He was on earth. What is He praying in heaven for them? For sure, there are some general and specific aspects

189

of His prayers. For instance, He is praying for us to be holy, not happy: "Be holy yourselves also in all your behavior; because it is written, 'You shall be holy for I am holy'" (1 Pet. 1:15–16). He is praying for us to "not be conformed to this world, but be transformed by the renewing of your mind, so that you may prove what the will of God is, that which is good and acceptable and perfect" (Rom. 12:2). Without this continual renewing of the mind, the believer cannot know the will of God. Jesus' words in John 15 reveal even more of His prayers on our behalf. He prays we would abide in Him; bear fruit, more fruit, and much fruit and that this fruit will remain; and love one another. And in His high priestly prayer of John 17 we know Jesus prays to the Father to keep us from the evil one, to sanctify us in the truth, to have oneness in Christ, and to display a genuine love for the Father and Son such that the world would be able to see it. This list of what He is praying for us, in general, is very long.

However, we do know that He prays specifically for us as well. In Luke 22:31–32, we have recorded Jesus' specific prayer for Peter: "Simon, Simon, behold, Satan has demanded permission to sift you like wheat; but I have prayed for you, that your faith may not fail; and you, when once you have turned again, strengthen your brothers."

Jesus in His omniscience knew that Peter was going to fail, and such failures can greatly sidetrack a believer or even detour them in their walk in Christ. Jesus' specific prayer was (1) that Peter's faith would not fail, (2) that Peter would turn back to the Lord again, and (3) that he would strengthen his Christian brothers. All that Jesus prayed was answered (see a whole chapter on this prayer.[2] The specificity of this prayer should be an extreme encouragement to all believers since we all fail, we all make mistakes, we all will experience some devastating trials, and we all have successes which can easily destroy us. "He always lives to make intercession" for us. Be encouraged!

REFLECT AND APPLY

1. "The will of God is always best, whatever the circumstances." That usually means the cross first followed by the crown in God's time as modeled by our Lord and Savior. Why do so many Christians continue to try to avoid the cross in route to the crown? Does that avoidance affect our prayer life? Spend one day next week asking God to show you how you have tried to avoid the unique cross God has for you. If no answer, come back the next week and repeat. If such avoidances are evident in your walk, confess, accept God's cleansing, and ask Him to fill you with His Spirit to start anew.

2. "He was praying for them in their ignorance and in their confusion, praying to the heavenly Father for His sheep. And that is exactly what He is doing now!" No matter what pain, chaos, frustration, stagnancy, failure, detour, loss, or trial we are currently or have previously experienced, He knows about it. He is praying for us to respond in such a way that there is glory to God and that people will be drawn to Christ through our response. Reflect on some past difficult experiences where you may have felt that God was distant. Apply the truth that He is always praying for us to that past experience. Use this truth of His always praying for us to free you to rest in His will.

3. In the context of Jesus always praying for us, the Scriptures tell us that He prays in specific areas. First, *He doesn't want our faith to fail*, no matter what the trial or storm we are going through. Second, He in His omniscience knows that these storms can shipwreck lives and lead us astray, but they can also purify our faith. So *He wants us to see our trials as allowed by God for our good*. Third, *He wants these storms or trials to strengthen our faith and be a backdrop for strengthening our brothers and sisters in Christ*. Reflect back to some past storms or difficult trials in your life during the past year, and ask yourself if your faith was strengthened and if the experience was a springboard to richer ministry in the lives of others. If your response was poor, ask God for grace and strength to respond biblically correct next time. If your response was correct, ask God how you could have responded better.

PREPARE BY PRAYER: PART 1

Then saith Jesus unto them, All ye shall be offended because of me this night: for it is written, I will smite the shepherd, and the sheep of the flock shall be scattered abroad. But after I am risen again, I will go before you into Galilee. Peter answered and said unto him, Though all men shall be offended because of thee, yet will I never be offended. Jesus said unto him, Verily I say unto thee, That this night, before the cock crow, thou shalt deny me thrice. Peter said unto him, Though I should die with thee, yet will I not deny thee. Likewise also said all the disciples. Then cometh Jesus with them unto a place called Gethsemane, and saith unto the disciples, Sit ye here, while I go and pray yonder. And he took with him Peter and the two sons of Zebedee, and began to be sorrowful and very heavy. Then saith he unto them, My soul is exceeding sorrowful, even unto death: tarry ye here, and watch with me. And he went a little farther, and fell on his face, and prayed, saying, O my Father, if it be possible, let this cup pass from me: nevertheless not as I will, but as thou wilt. And he cometh unto the disciples, and findeth them asleep, and saith unto Peter, What, could ye not watch with me one hour? Watch and pray, that ye enter not into temptation: the spirit indeed is willing, but the flesh is weak. —Matthew 26:31–41

That which immediately precedes and follows Matthew 26:41, "Watch and pray, that ye enter not into temptation: the spirit indeed is willing, but the flesh is weak," is the record of the most critical event in the history of the world. There can be no doubt of that at all, that it had about it and upon it more mighty historic significance, greater human weight of woe than any other event or series of events in the history of mankind.

The Lord Jesus Christ, the Redeemer of men, was about to be betrayed into the hands of sinners. He was about to offer His holy soul, to have poured out upon that soul the accumulated putrefaction and moral filth of the whole race of man, and to carry it to the tree and die there in agony and blood.

Now, there was one present, the one most vitally concerned, who anticipated this crisis and prepared for it. That one, of course, was Jesus, and He prepared for it by the most effective preparation known in heaven or in earth, namely prayer in the garden of Gethsemane. Let us not pity our Lord, as some are inclined to do. Let us thank Him that He first saw the crisis, and that He went to the place of power and the source of energy and got Himself ready for that event.

Because He did this, He passed the cosmic crisis triumphantly. One would say "cosmic crisis" because it had to do with more than this world. It had to do with more even than the human race. It had to do with the entire cosmos, the whole wide universe; for the Lord was dying that all things might be united in Him and that the heavens as well as the earth might be purged, and that new heavens and a new earth might be established that could never pass away.

All this rested upon the shoulders of the Son of God here this night in the garden, and He got ready for this in the most effective way known under the sun, and that is by going to God in prayer. But over against that were His disciples. They approached the crisis without anticipation. Partly, they did not know; partly, they did not care. Partly, they were too unspiritual to be concerned and partly they were sleepy. So, carelessly and prayerlessly and sleepily, they allowed themselves to be carried by the rolling of the wheel of time into a crisis so vital, so portentous that nothing like it has ever happened in the world and never will happen again. The result of their failure to anticipate was that one betrayed our Lord, one denied our Lord, and all forsook our Lord, fleeing away.

Christ gave those disciples then—and to disciples today— these words as a sort of a little diamond set in this great ring: "Watch and pray that ye enter not into temptation for the spirit indeed is willing but the flesh is weak." I want you to know that this prayer that Jesus made that night in the garden was an anticipatory prayer. That is, He prayed in anticipation of something that He knew was coming in the will of God, and He got ready for it. Now this is what I want to emphasize and lay upon your conscience that you practice anticipatory prayer because battles are lost before they are fought.

You can write that line across your memory, and history of the world and biography will support it: battles are always lost before they are fought. It was true and is true of nations across time as it was true of Israel.

Back in the Old Testament times you would find that when Israel went in righteous and prayed up, she never lost a battle. But when she went in filled with iniquity and prayerlessness, she never won a battle. The people always lost a battle when they worshiped the golden calf or sat down to eat and drink and rose up to play or when they intermarried with the nations or when they neglected the altar of Jehovah and raised up a heathen altar under some tree. It was then that Israel lost the battle. And so it was by anticipation, the battle was lost before it happened.

It was true of the disciples here in Gesthemane. They didn't lose in the morning when one of them cursed and said he was not a disciple. When even John, who loved Him, forsook Him and fled and every disciple sneaked away and melted into the night, that was not when the collapse came. The collapse had started the night before when, tired and weary, [three of the disciples] lay down and slept instead of listening to the voice of their Savior and staying awake to pray. If they had stayed awake and prayed alongside Him and heard His groans and seen His bloody sweat, it might've changed the history of the world, and certainly it would have changed their history.

Not only are battles lost before they are fought, battles are also won before they are fought. Look at David and Goliath. Everyone knows the story; we tell it to the children and the artists paint it, and it has got a place in the thoughts and literature of all the world, how little David with his ruddy cheeks went out and slew the mighty, roaring, breast-beating giant, almost ten feet tall and with a sword like a weaver's beam. And yet, tiny little stripling David went out and, with one stone, laid him down low, and with his own great sword which David could hardly lift, cut off and carried that huge head by the hair and displayed it before a shouting, triumphant Israel. When did David win that battle? When did he win that fight? When he walked quietly out to meet that great, boasting giant? No!

Let somebody else try it and the words of Goliath would have been proved true. "I'll tear you to pieces and feed you to the birds," he said. And under other circumstances, he'd have done just that but David was a young man who knew God, and he had slain the lion and the bear, and he had taken his sheep as the very charge of the Almighty. He had prayed and meditated and lain under the stars at night and talked to God and had learned that when God sends a man, that man can conquer any enemy, no matter how strong. So it was not that morning on the plain there between the two hills that David won; it was all down the years to his boyhood, when his mother taught him to pray and he learned to know God for himself.

Then there was Jacob who, after twenty years, prepared to meet his angry brother who had threatened to kill him. He had never seen him; he had gotten away so that Esau couldn't kill him, and now Jacob was coming back. The Lord revealed that the next day the brothers would meet on the plain beyond the Jabok River. The next day, they met down on the plain—and they threw themselves into each other's arms, and Esau forgave Jacob, and Jacob conquered his brother's ire and his brother's murderous intent. When did Jacob do it? Did he do it that morning when he walked out to meet his brother and crossed over the river? No! He did it the night before when he wrestled alone with his God. It was then he prepared himself to conquer Esau—the sulky, solemn, and hairy man of the forest who had solemnly threatened after the oriental oath that he would slay Jacob when he found him.

How could he cancel that oath? How could he violate the salty oath taken after the manner of the East? God Almighty took it out of his heart when Jacob wrestled alone by the river. Always it's so, and Jacob conquered Esau the night before; not when they met but the night before they met.

It was also so with Elijah. Elijah defeated Ahab and Jezebel and all the prophets of Baal and brought victory and revival to Israel (in 1 Kings 18). And when did he do it? Did he do it that day on Carmel? After the prophets of Baal all day long had prayed and leaped on the altar and cut themselves until they were bloody, then Elijah walked up at 6 o'clock in the evening, at the time of the evening sacrifice. Elijah walked up and prayed a little prayer. Was it a prayer that took him twenty minutes as we sometimes do in prayer meetings and shut ours off? Was it a long, eloquent prayer? No, it was a blunt, brief, little prayer of exactly sixty-two words in English (and I would assume fewer in Hebrew). So there was your prayer. Did that prayer bring down the fire? Yes and no. Yes, because if it hadn't been offered, there would have been no fire. No, because if Elijah hadn't known God all back down the years and hadn't stood before God during the long days and months and years that preceded Carmel, that prayer would have collapsed by its own weight, and they would have torn Elijah to pieces.

So it was not on Mt. Carmel that Baal was defeated; it was at Mt. Gilead. Remember that it was from Gilead that Elijah came. That great, shaggy, hairy man dressed in the simple rustic garb of the peasants came down, boldly staring straight ahead and without any court manners or any knowledge of how to talk or what to do. He walked straight in, smelling of the mountain and the fields, and stood before the cowardly, henpecked Ahab and said, "I am Elijah. I stand before Jehovah. And I'm just here to tell you there will be no rain until I say so. Goodbye."

That was a dramatic moment, a terrible moment, a wonderful moment, but back of that, were long, long years of standing before Jehovah. Elijah didn't know he was to be sent to the court of Ahab, but he had anticipated it by long prayers and waiting and meditations in the presence of his God.

Edited sermon presented on June 9, 1957,
at Southwest Alliance Church, Chicago

REFLECT AND APPLY

1. The disciples approached the crisis in the garden of Gethsemane without anticipation. "Partly, they didn't know; partly, they didn't care. Partly, they were too unspiritual to be concerned and partly they were sleepy." Do we not do likewise today over and over? Roots of our failures in anticipation can be found in insufficient practical knowledge of the Scriptures, lack of practice of the truth, poor discernment, pushings from the world, and pulls

of the flesh. Honestly evaluate some crisis that you experienced in the past year. If you stumbled in the crisis, what were the causes of the missteps? If you succeeded in the crisis, what were root causes of that success? In either case, did you anticipate the crisis? What did you learn about prayer as a result of failure or success in the crisis?

2. "He (Jesus) prayed in anticipation of something that He knew was coming in the will of God, and He got ready for it. Now, this is what I want to emphasize and lay upon your conscience that you practice anticipatory prayer because battles are lost before they are fought." How do we cultivate the practice of anticipatory prayer on a daily basis?

3. "The collapse [of the disciples] had started the night before when, tired and weary, they lay down and slept instead of listening to the voice of their Savior and staying awake to pray." Tiredness, sleepiness, praylessness, disappointment, and weakness in the spiritual disciplines undermine our prayer life and especially anticipatory prayer. Over the past thirty days, reflect in the power of the Holy Spirit about what things have undermined your praying as Tozer recommends. Repent and ask God for assistance from this day forward in reviving your prayer life.

4. David faced a giant (Goliath) crisis, Jacob faced a family crisis, and Elijah faced a national crisis of Baal worship. It is part of life that we will all face personal, family, and national crises. Over the past

few years, what has been your response in such crises? In a body of believers, do you learn from the crises of others? From this point forward, how will you face the crises to come? Be specific!

27

PREPARE BY PRAYER: PART 2

There are crises that wait for us out there, even as there was a crisis that faced Jesus and His disciples, David and Israel, and Elijah and all the rest. Crises wait for us; I want to name a few of them briefly.

The first of them is *acute trouble*. The history of the human race shows that it comes to us all at some time. When sharp trouble with its shocking, weakening sting comes to us, some Christians meet it unprepared. And of course, they collapse.

But is it the trouble that brings the collapse? Yes and no. It is the trouble that brings the collapse in that they wouldn't have collapsed without the trouble. But it is not the trouble that causes them to collapse, because if they had anticipated it and prepared for it, they would not have collapsed. "Man who goes down into trouble," says the proverb; "his strength is small." And his strength is small because his prayers are few and lean.

But the man whose prayers are many and strong will not collapse when the trouble comes.

Second, there is *temptation*—temptation that comes unexpected and subtle, and it's too unexpected and too subtle for the flesh. But anticipatory prayer gets the soul ready for whatever temptation there may be. Was it the day that David walked on the rooftop that he fell into his disgraceful and tragic temptation? No! It was his long gap that the historians say was in between, and they don't know what David was doing. I know one thing David wasn't doing; he wasn't waiting on his God. He wasn't out looking at the stars and saying, "The heavens declare the glory of God." He did that, but there was a time he was not doing it. And so David went down because the whole weight of his wasted weeks before bore down upon him. Temptation can't hurt you if you have anticipated it by prayer, but temptation will certain fell you if you have not.

Third, there are *Satan's attacks*. Now, Satan's attacks are rarely anticipated because Satan is too shrewd to be uniform. You see, if Satan established a pattern of attack, we'd soon catch on to his pattern. If the devil were to be regular in his attacks, the human race would have found him out a long time ago, and the poorest old church member would've known how to avoid him. But because he is not uniform but highly irregular and mixes things up, he is deadly if we haven't the shield of faith to protect ourselves.

Take a baseball pitcher, for instance. He doesn't start throwing when the first inning begins and throw the same ball in the same place for nine innings. If he did, the score would be 128 to nothing. What does he do? He mixes them up. The batter never knows where they're going to appear. First up, then down, then in, then out, then low, then fast, then down the middle; he mixes them up. It is the absence of uniformity that makes the pitcher effective. Do you think the devil isn't as smart as the best major league pitcher?

Do you think the devil doesn't know that the way to win over a Christian is to fool him by irregularity? Never attack him twice the same way in the same day.

He's coming in from one side one time, another side another time, like the boxer. Do you think that boxer goes in there and gets himself rigidly stereotyped? He leads with his left; he strikes with his right; he moves back two steps; he moves forward two steps. Why, the most common stumblebum would win over a fighter like that. A fighter has to use his head too. First, he attacks from one side, then from another, then dashes in, then backs away, then pedals backwards, then charges, and then it's left, then right, then feints, then sidesteps, and then ducks, then weaves, then bobs. The devil doesn't come in always the same way. He'll come at you today like a wild bull of Beijing and tomorrow he'll be as soft as Ferdinand. And the next day, he won't bother you at all. Then he'll fight you three days in a row and let you alone for three weeks.

Remember what was said of Jesus after the three temptations? Satan left him for a season. Why? To get the Lord to drop His guard was the intention, of course. And so, the devil fights like a boxer. He uses strategy. That's why it is pretty hard to anticipate. You don't know what he's going to do next, but you can always put a blanket of anticipation down. You can always figure that the devil's after you. And so, by prayer and watching and waiting on God, you can be ready for his coming. When he does come, you can win! Not the day he arrives but the day before he arrives. Not the noon he gets to you but the morning before the noon.

The only way to win consistently, my brethren, is to keep the blood on the doorpost, keep the cloud and fire over you, keep your fighting clothes on you, and never allow a day to creep up on you. Never get up early in the morning, and look at your clock and say, "I'll miss my train" and dash away. If you must dash away, take a New Testament along. Instead of reading the local or national news, read your New Testament on your way to work, then bow your head and talk to God. Get ready for the battle! Rather than not pray at all, grab prayer somewhere in the morning.

My recommendation is to never let a day creep up on you. Never let Thursday worry you because you didn't pray on Wednesday. Never let Tuesday get you down because you were prayerless on Monday. Never let 3 o'clock in the afternoon floor you because you didn't pray at 7 in the morning. See that you get prayed up somewhere.

In conclusion, I have four recommendations. First, never act as if things were all right. Now, if the devil lets you alone awhile, you're not in much trouble, you're reasonably happy and reasonably spiritual, you're likely to say, "Well, things are all right," and you'll neglect your prayer life and you don't watch and pray. Remember, as long as sin and the devil and disease and death are abroad in the land like a virus, like a contagious disease, things are not all right. We're not living in a wholesome world, a world that is geared to keep you spiritually healthy. This vile world is not a friend of grace to lead us on to God. It's the opposite. So instead of assuming that things are all right, assume that they're always wrong and then prepare for them and anticipate them from whatever direction they come.

The second recommendation is never trust the devil and say things are all right. Just as you can't trust a communist, you can't trust the devil. Never imagine that he's smiling. Never look at the picture of him by Doré or somebody and say, "Oh, he's not a bad-looking devil. Perhaps all this is more or less just like Santa Claus and Jack Frost; it's only imaginary." Never trust the devil. Always anticipate any possible attack by watching and praying for the Spirit. Though the flesh is willing, it is terribly weak.

Third, never become overconfident for the very reason that our Lord stated, "The flesh is weak." Never become overconfident! Many a man has lost a fight from overconfidence. Many a businessman has lost a business because he was overconfident.

And fourth, never underestimate the power of prayer. "Watch and pray," said Jesus, and He wasn't talking poetry. "Watch and pray," said Jesus, and He practiced it and won because He did practice it. He caught the spinning world that sin had thrown out of gear, caught them in the web of His own love and redeemed them with the shedding of His own blood. He did it, I say, because He readied Himself for that awful event and that glorious event by prayer the night before, and by prayer in the mountains at other times and by prayer down the years through His boyhood. Never underestimate the power of prayer. Remember that without it you cannot win, and with it you cannot lose, granted, of course, that it's true prayer and not saying of words; granted your life is in harmony with your prayer. If you pray, you cannot lose, and if you fail to pray, you cannot win.

The Lord gave us the example of anticipatory prayer—getting

ready for any event by seeking the face of God in watchful prayer at regular times. Practice anticipatory prayer. Then no matter what happens, like Jesus Christ our Lord, like Daniel, Elijah, and the rest, you can go triumphantly through, for prayer always wins.

Edited sermon presented on June 9, 1957, at Southwest Alliance Church, Chicago

REFLECT AND APPLY

1. Acute troubles, temptations, and Satan's attacks, just in broad categories, represent seven combinations of crises: all three at the same time, each one at a separate time, or three pairs of the crises. Then if one considers all the types of acute troubles, temptations, and satanic attacks, there is no way in the power of the flesh that we can be prepared for the variety and irregularity of the crises that come our way. It is a must that we prepare by prayer every day. Reflect back over the past week or month as to what acute troubles, temptations, or satanic attacks have come your way. Did you recognize or discern the crises before the fact or after the fact? What was your prayer status the day or week before? What have you learned now about being prepared by prayer for such crises?

2. Tozer made recommendations as to anticipatory prayer. The first two were "never act as if things were all right" and "never trust the devil and say

things are all right." Appearances are always deceiving. Paul warns us of taking "pride in appearance and not in heart" (2 Cor. 5:12) or of "looking at things as they are outwardly" (2 Cor. 10:7). These perspectives hold not only for the individual but also a body of believers. Remember how the elders and leaders of Israel reasoned by the outward appearances of the Gibeonites (Joshua 8) and did not seek the Lord's counsel. We do likewise even today. How does one avoid being swept up in the appearances of a situation instead of the reality? Where does Ephesians 6:10–11 ("Be strong in the Lord and in the strength of His might. Put on the full armor of God, so that you will be able to stand firm against the schemes of the devil") fit in dealing with appearances or saying things are all right?

3. Overconfidence is a very real hindrance to anticipatory prayer. What breeds this overconfidence: our past successes, our supposed maturity in Christ, our station in life, our education, our self-discipline or self-control, our most recent success, or maybe a seemingly lull in the satanic attacks and crises? Tozer rightly notes that the ultimate source of this overconfidence is our flesh. The apostle Paul talks about his confidence in the flesh and his solution in Philippians 3:2–16. Take his solution and apply it to your life with specifics.

4. "Never underestimate the power of prayer." In what ways do we underestimate the power of prayer? Is it in praying little, praying inconsistently, praying only when a crisis comes along, praying only when no other solution is feasible, praying

only when there is time or it is convenient, praying only when we are not tired, praying only about major trials or life events, or more? Identify the excuses or situations that have caused you to underestimate the power of prayer. Confess and ask God to help you avoid underestimating the power of prayer!

28

BELIEVING PRAYER

Let me say that there is a great deal of praying being done that doesn't amount to anything. It never brings anything back to us. There is no possible good in trying to cover up this fact or to deny it. We would do a great lot better by admitting that there is enough prayer made any Sunday to save the whole world, even four or five suburbs of the world. But the world isn't saved and much of our praying is the echo of our own voices.

This has a very injurious effect upon the church of Christ— not only injurious but sometimes disastrous. Unanswered prayer does five things in a congregation over an extended time.

First, it tends to chill and discourage the praying people. If we continue to ask like a petulant child that doesn't expect to get what he asks for but continues to whine for it and if we continue to do that and never get an answer, the temptation is that we will get chilled and cold inside our hearts and become discouraged.

Then it confirms the natural unbelief of the heart. For remember this—the human heart is filled with unbelief. It was unbelief that led to the first act of disobedience. Therefore, not disobedience but unbelief was the first sin. While disobedience is the first recorded sin, in back of the act of disobedience there was the sin of unbelief. Otherwise, the disobedience would never have taken place. As a result, here is the danger I see. To pray and not receive an answer and to have a church pray and never see the answer is detrimental to solid spiritual growth. When we pray for the sick and have them not recover or even die, when we pray for deliverance and never see it, when we pray for a thousand things and never see one of them brought to pass, I would say the effect is to confirm the natural unbelief in the human heart.

Third, unanswered prayer encourages the idea that religion is unreal. A great many people already have the idea that religion is unreal. They believe that it is a subjective thing purely, that there is nothing real about it, and that there is nothing to which it can be referred. For instance, if I use the word "lake," everybody thinks of a large body of water. I use the word "star," and everybody thinks of the heavenly bodies. But if I use the words "faith," "belief," "God," or "heaven," there is nothing to which they refer. They are just words, which like pixies and fairies and such things that have no reference in the real world.

The next step in the regression is plenty of occasions for the enemy to blaspheme. The enemy, the devil, loves to blaspheme. He is a dirty-mouth, obscene blasphemer. I have a lot of secret sympathy for that rough old Irishman William Nicholson, who calls the devil "a dirty ole pig." And he is an obscene old pig that loves to blaspheme. If he can get a lot of Christians howling to high heaven for weeks on end and see to it that they never get an answer, then he has more obscenities to voice plus he blasphemes God even more.

Worst of all, it lets the enemy take possession of the field. In the failure of a military drive, the worst part is not the men they lose. The worst part is not the face they lose. The worst part of the failure of a military drive is that it leaves the enemy in possession of the field.

Thus, when the people of God pray and pray and get nowhere, it leaves the enemy in possession of the field. This, in itself, is a great tragedy and a disaster. The devil should be on the run. We should never see anything but the back of his neck. He should always be retreating and retreating, and his worst fighting should be rear-guard action, scorched-earth policy, burning, and destroying as he goes. He should always be on the run. Instead of that, the obscene and blasphemous enemy smugly and scornfully holds his position, and the people of God let him have it. This, of course, retards the work of the Lord greatly.

Having no prayers answered—having prayers sent up to heaven that come back empty—is like sending an army out without weapons. It is like a pianist trying to play without fingers. It is like sending a woodsman without an axe into the woods. It is like sending a farmer without a plow into the field. The work of God stands still in such situations.

Now, Jesus said that we could have anything we ask for in His name (John 14:13–14; 1 John 5:14–15). The apostle John said that this is the confidence, the boldness, and the assurance which we have in Him. The man of unfaith rejects flatly this kind of teaching and demands the proof of human reason. This man without faith says, "I've got to have a reason for this." The man of faith feels confidence and dares not rest upon human reasoning. Or to put it another way, I have used reason to do what reason can do—mainly to show that there are some things that reason cannot do. I have never been against human reason, but I have been against human reason trying to do things human reason is not qualified to do.

The great difference today in the world is not between the liberal and the fundamentalist. The great gulf fixed today is between the evangelical rationalist and the evangelical mystic. The evangelical rationalists insist upon trying to reduce everything down to where it can be explained and proved and thus have rationalized faith and have pulled the Almighty God down to the low level of human reason. On the other hand, the evangelical mystic believes God and disbelieves human reason since there are some things human reason cannot do.

Human reason and faith are not contrary to each other, but one is above the other. When we are believers, we enter another world altogether, a realm that is infinitely above little reason. "My thoughts are not your thoughts nor are your ways My ways, saith the Lord. For as the heavens are higher than the earth, so are my ways higher than your ways and my thoughts, than your thoughts" (Isa. 55:8–9). Faith never goes contrary to reason; faith simply ignores reason and rises above it.

For instance, reason could not tell us that Jesus Christ should be born of the Virgin Mary, but faith knows He was. Reason cannot prove that Jesus took upon Him the form of a man and died under the sins of the world, but faith knows He did. Reason cannot prove that the third day He rose from the dead, but faith knows that He did. Thus, reason doesn't know these things, but faith does: faith is an organ of knowledge.

Faith is the highest kind of reason. Faith takes us straight into

214

the presence of God and goes behind the veil where our Lord Jesus Christ, our Forerunner, has gone for us, and engages God Almighty and reaches that for which He was ordained to do. It is here where the man of faith communes with the source of his being, loves the Fountain of his life, prays to the One who begot him, and knows the God who made heaven and earth. He may not be an astronomer, but he knows the God who made the stars. He may not be a physicist, but he knows the God who made mathematics.

There may be many technical and local bits of knowledge the man of faith doesn't have; but he knows the God of all knowledge, penetrates the veil into the Presence, stands hushed and wide-eyed, and gazes and gazes and gazes upon the wonders of deity. Faith takes him there! "If God says it, I know it's so! Why? "This is the confidence that we have in him" [1 John 5:14]. Reason cannot disprove anything that faith does. Not all the scientific facts ever assembled in any university of the world can support one spiritual fact since we are in two different realms or two different worlds: one deals with reason and the other deals with faith.

The promises of God, the character of Jesus' blood, and the character of God are the ground of our hope. Not our goodness! Not what we promise to do and not what we have done, but what He promises us. And He cannot lie through the merits of His Son. So if you are in any kind of trouble, why don't you go to God and put Him to the test? Get on your knees and pray it through. Pray it through! Will you do that?

If you have trouble in your home, trouble in your business, real trouble, go to God about it. Get down on your knees. Open your Bible and say, "God, I haven't thought about it, but I can trust Thee." Then look for the promises. God Almighty won't let you down. God will make the iron swim, and God will help out His children.

Edited sermon presented on August 21, 1955,
at Southwest Alliance Church, Chicago

─────────

REFLECT AND APPLY

1. "We would do a great lot better by admitting that there is enough prayer made any Sunday to save the whole world, even four or five suburbs of the world. But the world isn't saved and much of our praying is the echo of our own voices." Assess the reality of this Tozer quote as to your own church and to your own personal walk in Christ. Is there a lot of praying by your church and by you? What is the level of obedience to the Word of God in your church and in your own walk? One must always remember that prayer is no substitute for obedience, for "to obey is better than sacrifice" (1 Sam. 15:22).

2. Unanswered prayer does five things in a congregation over an extended time: (1) it tends to discourage the praying people; (2) it tends to confirm the natural unbelief of the heart; (3) it tends to encourage the idea that religion is unreal; (4) it gives occasions for the enemy to blaspheme; and (5) it lets the enemy take possession of the field. Which of these outcomes have been more apparent in

your church and in your life? Why do you think so? What must be done to reclaim the possession of the field in your circumstances? Seek the Lord for His unique answer to your situation.

3. At some time or maybe even much of the time, we have all been guilty of reducing things "down to where they can be explained and proved and thus have rationalized faith and have pulled the Almighty God down to the low level of human reason." Let's allow the Holy Spirit to search our hearts and minds to expose such worldly and fleshly perspectives. As He convicts, repent and ask God to enable you to walk by faith even more. Of course, this is not a one-time experience but one that we will need to repeat as necessary.

4. "Faith is the highest kind of reason. Faith takes us straight into the presence of God and goes behind the veil where our Lord Jesus Christ, our Forerunner, has gone for us, and engages God Almighty and reaches that for which He was ordained to do. It is here where the man of faith communes with the source of his being, loves the Fountain of his life, prays to the One who begot him, and knows the God who made heaven and earth." Find encouragement in this statement of Tozer for your current circumstances.

5. If you have trouble in your home, trouble in your business, real trouble, go to God about it. Get down on your knees. Open your Bible and say, "God, I haven't thought about it, but I can trust You." Then look for the promises. God Almighty won't let you down. . . . God will make the iron

swim, and God will help out His children." By faith, believe in Him and His Word. Identify such troubles that you are experiencing and lay them before the Lord God standing on the specific promises of His Word.

NOTES

Introduction: A Journey Awaits

1. A. W. Tozer, *The Counselor,* comp. Gerald B. Smith, rev. ed. (Camp Hill, PA: WingSpread, 1993), Database 2007, Word Search Corp., chap. 10.

Chapter 4: To Be Right, We Must Think Right

1. Earl Radmacher, *You and Your Thoughts: The Power of Right Thinking* (Tyndale ,1977; repr. Dallas, OR: Redeeming Press, 2014), n. p. This small book offers much insight into this battle for our minds.

Chapter 8: Praying without Condition

1. Ole Hallesby, trans. Clarence J. Carlsen, *Prayer* (Minneapolis: Augsburg, 1931), 27.

Chapter 9: The Power of Silence

1. A. W. Tozer, *Of God and Men* (Harrisburg, PA: Christian Publications, 1960), 103–04.
2. A. W. Tozer, *The Pursuit of God* (Camp Hill, PA: WingSpread Publishers, 2006), 76.
3. Ibid.

Chapter 10: Dangers in Unanswered Prayer

1. A. W. Tozer, *The Warfare of the Spirit* (Camp Hill, PA: WingSpread, 1993), 123.
2. For more on the topic see W. L. Seaver, *A Mosaic of Faith: 11 Lessons Jesus Taught His Disciples* (Camp Hill, PA: WingSpread, 2012).

Chapter 11: What Profit in Prayer?

1. F. I. Anderson, *Job*: Tyndale Old Testament Commentaries (Downers Grove, IL: InterVarsity, 1976), 19.

Chapter 12: Three Ways to Get What We Want

1. Herbert M. Carson, *The Epistles of Paul to the Colossians and Philemon* (Grand Rapids: Eerdmans, 1975), 95–96.

Chapter 15: Praying Till We Pray

1. D. A. Carson, *A Call to Spiritual Reformation* (Grand Rapids: Baker, 1992), 36.

Chapter 16: God's Selfhood and Prayer

1. Frederick William Faber, "Majesty Divine," *Faber's Hymns* (n.p., 1862; repr., Charleston, SC: BiblioLife, 2009), 5.

Chapter 18: Honesty in Prayer

1. David M'Intyre, *The Hidden Life of Prayer* (repr., Grand Rapids, Bethany, 1993), n.p.
2. François Fénelon, *Spiritual Letters of Archbishop Fénelon* (London: Rivingtons Water Place, 1877), 206.
3. A. W. Tozer, *Faith Beyond Reason* (Camp Hill, PA: WingSpread, 2012), chap. 3, "The Direction of the Mind," n.p.

Chapter 19: Measuring Spirituality by Public Prayers

1. Gary Inrig, *The Parables* (Grand Rapids: Discovery House, 1991), 166–69.

Chapter 20: The Best Things Come Hard

1. W. L. Seaver, *A Mosaic of Faith: 11 Lessons Jesus Taught His Disciples* (Camp Hill, PA: WingSpread, 2012), 123–51.

Chapter 21: A Word to the Men about the Women

1. E. M. Bounds, *Power through Prayer* (Grand Rapids: Baker, 1972), 7.

Chapter 22: Does God Always Answer Prayer?

1. A. W. Tozer, *The Root of the Righteous* (Camp Hill, PA: WingSpread, 2006), 124.

Chapter 23: Vague Praying and Expectation

1. A. W. Tozer, *Success and the Christian,* comp. James L. Snyder (Camp Hill, PA: Christian Publications, 1994), 99–100.
2. Andrew Murray, *With Christ in the School of Prayer* (repr., Old Tappan, N.J., Fleming H. Revell, 1975), 56.

Chapter 24: In Everything by Prayer

1. A. W. Tozer, *The Tozer Pulpit, Volume One*, comp. Gerald B. Smith, Zur Ltd. Database © 2007 WORD*search* Corp. The original title was "How to Keep from Having a Nervous Breakdown." Also found in A. W. Tozer, *Renewed Day by Day*, comp. Gerald B. Smith (Camp Hill, PA, Christian Publications, Inc., 1980), Nov. 9.
2. A. W. Tozer, "In Everything by Prayer," *The Tozer Pulpit*, ed. James L. Snyder (Alachua, FL: Bridge-Logos, 2006), 41–55.

Chapter 25: Jesus Lives to Make Intercession for Us

1. A. W. Tozer, *Faith Beyond Reason* (1989; repr., Camp Hill, PA: WingSpread, 2009), 150–51. This sermon originally appeared as "God's Will Is Always Best" in the chapter titled "The Church Is on a Stormy Sea."
2. W. L. Seaver, *A Mosaic of Faith* (Camp Hill, PA: WingSpread Publishers, 2012), 217–38.

More from A. W. Tozer:

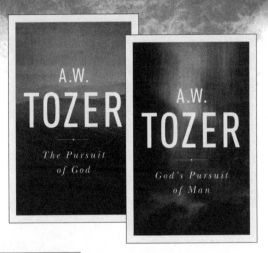

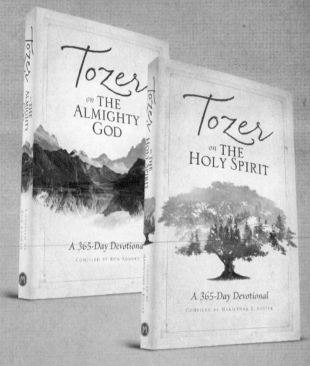

TITLES BY A.W. TOZER

*From the Word **to Life***

Moody Radio produces and delivers compelling programs filled with biblical insights and creative expressions of faith that help you take the next step in your relationship with Christ.

You can hear Moody Radio on 36 stations and more than 1,500 radio outlets across the U.S. and Canada. Or listen on your smartphone with the Moody Radio app!

www.moodyradio.org